Reflexology
an introduction

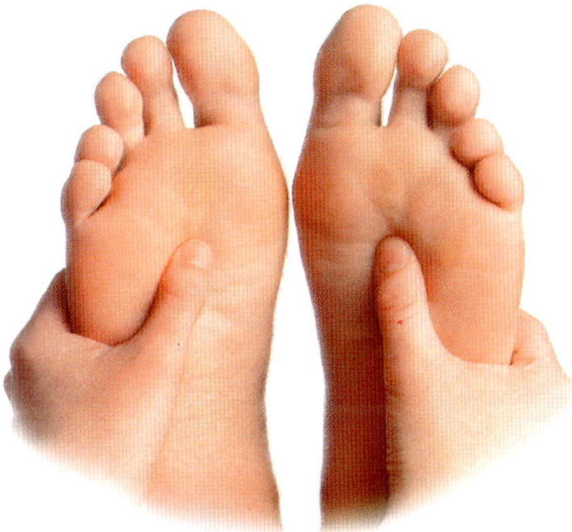

Written by Clare Macfarlane

LLYFRAU 'R YNYS
ISLAND BOOKS
PRODUCED FOR S. WEBB & SON
Menai Bridge

This edition published by Island Books, a division of S. Webb & Son, Telford Place, Pentraeth Road, Menai Bridge, Isle of Anglesey. LL59 5RW

Contents

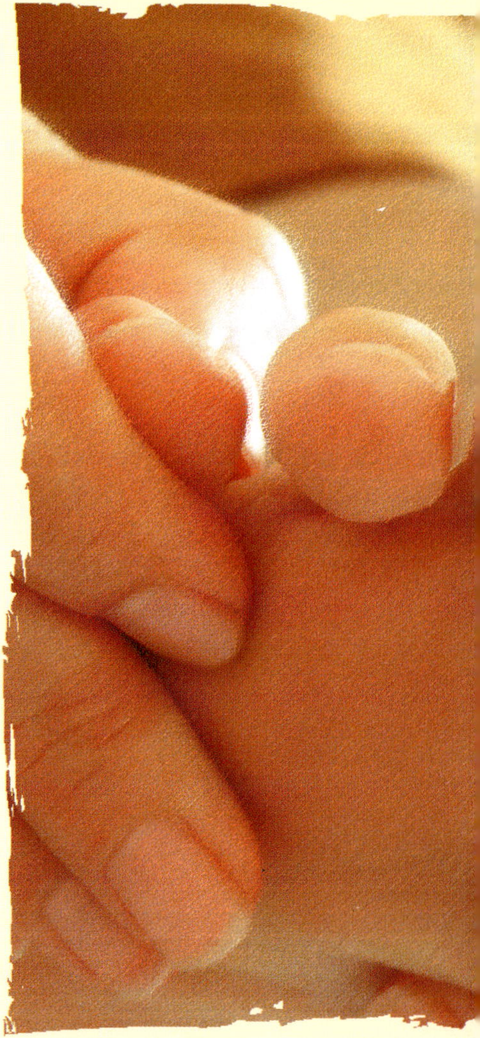

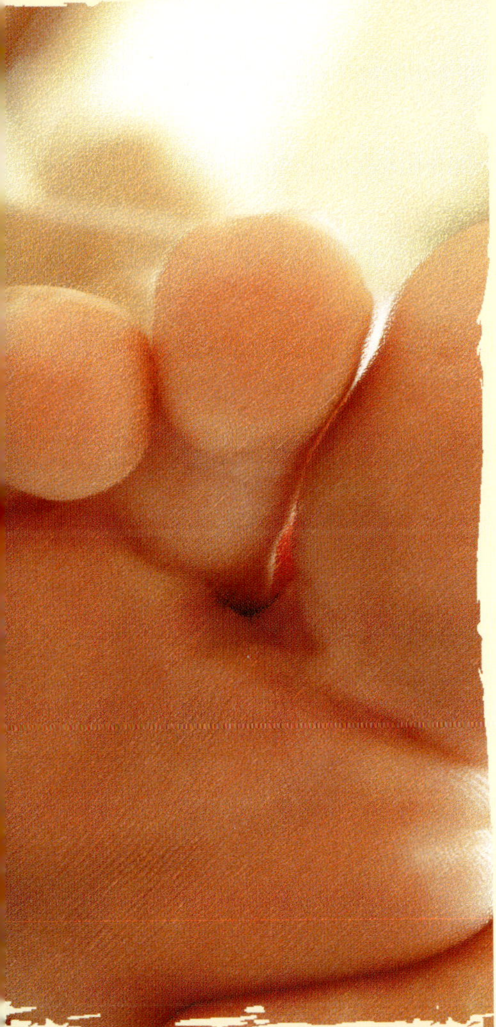

An INTRODUCTION to reflexology

Over the past few years reflexology, along with many other forms of complementary healthcare, has become increasingly popular with the general public.

There are many reasons for this surge in public interest and they reveal a great deal about the nature of our society today and the way in which we are forced to live our lives.

Firstly, as our lives become increasingly busy and hectic with work and home life, and as pressure takes its toll on the mind and body, reflexology offers a relief from those factors. It gives us time to relax and recharge our batteries, perhaps even allowing us the time to look within and redefine ourselves, our needs, dreams and desires.

Secondly, we live in an age where a lot of people have grown disillusioned with orthodox medicine and its disorganised treatment of the individual.

There are good doctors out there, but they have to work in a system that is not sympathetic to the needs and requirements of the patient. Many people have found that reflexology, along with other therapies, can help alleviate pain and symptoms of illness, attempting to balance the individual from a holistic point of view, and can provide relief to a swamped health service and its patients.

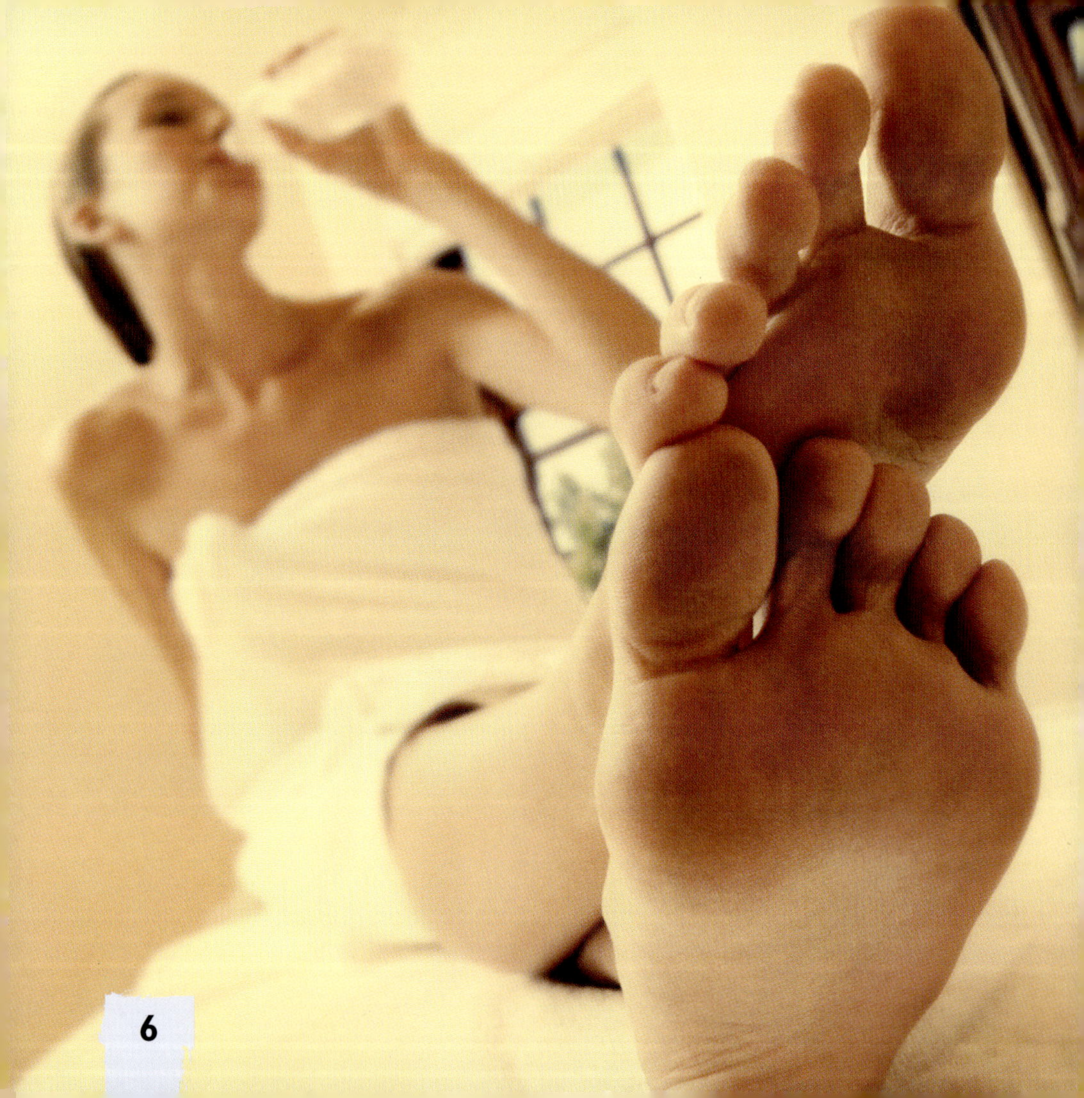

We are living in a fast paced, high-tech age, with business and economies, commitments and appointments ruling our lives. It is time we all slowed to a manageable pace and allowed ourselves the space to find our own happiness and nurture our lives.

Reflexology and other complementary therapies allow us to have that arena for a short space of time. It can allow a realisation to grow within us that perhaps our own lives are a bit more sacred than we had previously thought. So often we ignore our own needs and find ourselves doing everything for everyone else yet nothing for ourselves. It is important that we nurture our own being in order to keep our mind and body strong and healthy.

Reflexology looks at health and well-being from a holistic point of view, seeing the body as a system of parts and looking to correct any imbalance that may have occurred while acknowledging that the physical manifestation of illness or disease may be emotional, psychological or energetic in nature.

For example, each of us responds differently to a cold or flu germ that travels on the breeze, or from office to office. Some people may have just a sniffle while others are off work for days. Therefore, illness can be seen as being subjective, affecting the individual according to their weaknesses and points of stress and their emotional and psychological attitudes to their life.

The aim of this book is to give you a basic grounding in reflexology, providing guidance and instruction on how to give some basic treatment in order to help yourself, your friends and family. The first part deals with the history of this therapy, along with an explanation of how reflexology works, while the second part looks at how you can easily treat common ailments using simple step-by-step routines.

Historical **roots**

Reflexology has its basis in many ancient cultures, which practised a form of reflexology to improve a person's connection with Earth and its energies.

The form that is practised now is much more defined and exacting, focusing more on the effect on the physical being but recognised as being very influential on all aspects of the person.

From Ancient Egypt

The oldest evidence of practice was found in Saqqara, Egypt, within the tomb of a vizier known as Ankhmahor, which has been dated somewhere around the time of 2500–2330 BC. It depicts two people giving treatment and two receiving, and conveys the relationship between the stimulation of points on the feet and hands and the physical response.

The Inca civilisation is thought to have practised and passed their methods onto the Native American Indian tribes. The Cherokee Indians of North Carolina claim that this method of treatment has been with them and practised for centuries to the benefit of the tribe as a whole.

The Eastern method of practice, established in India and China, recognised that the feet were an excellent way of accessing and positively affecting the energy meridians within the body. These carry the body's life force and connect the individual to the universe and its energies. It is theorised that through the investigation into the location of pressure points, the practice of acupuncture was developed and honed as a skill.

Reflex Areas

From the more ancient civilisations, further study was developed by individuals who found that areas of the body were connected and could be affected by the application of pressure to alleviate pain and symptoms of illness. These points became known as reflex areas.

The direct link between the massage of painful areas for relief of problem areas elsewhere within the body was made by Dr Alfons Cornelius. He applied the use of massage to pressure points to help patients within his own practice. Sir Henry Head also discovered that areas of skin showed hypersensitivity to

pressure when an organ, or area of the body connected by nerves to the sensitive area, was diseased.

Zone Therapy

The most notable and documented person in establishing reflex zones was Dr William Fitzgerald who founded the practice of 'Zone Therapy'. Fitzgerald is credited with the discovery that pressure applied to certain areas of the body could have an anaesthetic-like effect on other parts.

After studying and furthering the work of Dr Bressler and as a result of his own investigations within practice, ten longitudinal zones were identified which are of equal distance within the body. It is within these zones that energy and physical matter can be affected by the use of pressure.

Mother of Reflexology

It was an interest in Fitzgerald's work that inspired Eunice Ingham, who separated the practice of zone therapy to the working of and development of the locations of organs and body parts to the feet, recognising that they are a sensitive and reflexive area of the body.

Ingham is referred to as 'the mother of Reflexology' for she was first to form a map that related the positions of organs and body parts to the feet. It is from her vision that many more specific and detailed maps have been developed. She also encouraged people to practise the techniques of reflexology for the benefit of others, as she saw the positive effect it had on people's lives through her own methods of practice.

Ingham's, nephew, Dwight Byers, used as a guinea pig in her pioneering work, has continued to bring this therapy into recognition, ensuring techniques and training are passed on by running the International Institute of Reflexology in St. Petersburg, USA.

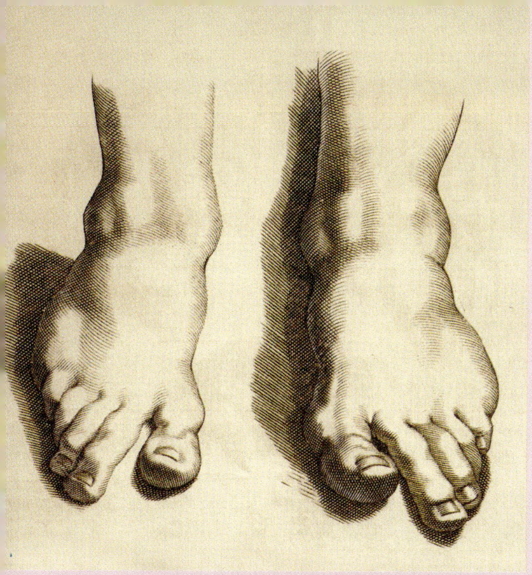

There are many people bringing their own knowledge and expertise to further the understanding and development of the practice of reflexology. Concentrating much more on the energetic and metaphysical aspects of practice, they are making the treatment more refined, encompassing the subtle form of the body.

Lynne Booth has developed a technique known as Vertical Reflexology Treatment (VRT), a new method of practice which accelerates the energetic healing process. Inge Dougans concentrates on the involvement and relevance of energy meridians in treatment. Anthony Porter has developed a system of Advanced Reflexology Techniques (ART) which helps further define and specify the focus of treatment, while many others are adding their own influence and contribution to the development of the therapy to make its application more thorough and effective.

Much more research and development is taking place to further investigate the way in which reflexology works while also exploring its effectiveness in treating a vast collection of conditions, illnesses and states of being.

It is the strong roots of this therapy and the commitment to its development by certain individuals that makes reflexology the effective practice that it is today.

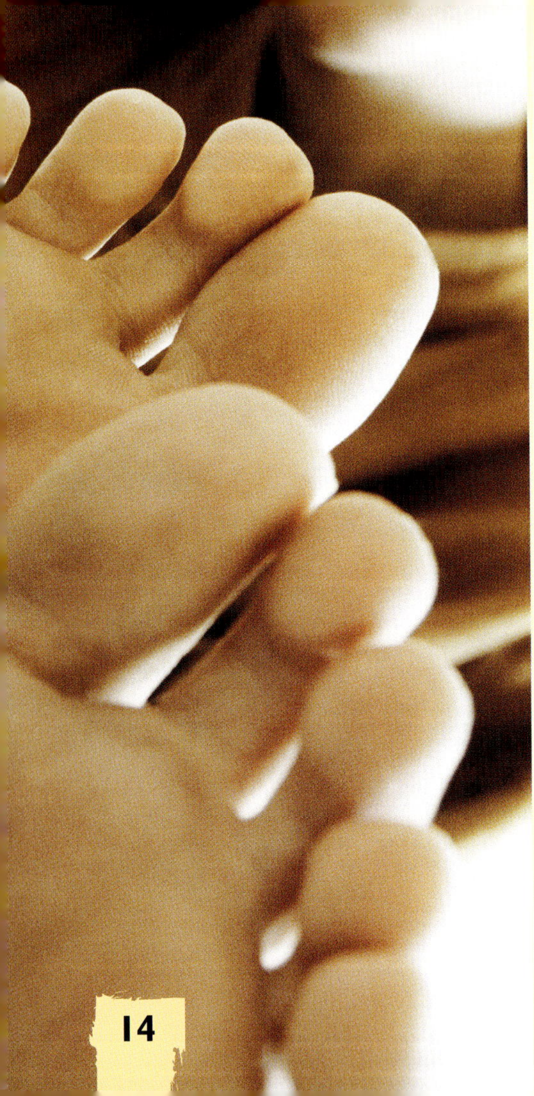

WHAT is reflexology?

Reflexology is a gentle, soothing, yet effective therapy, which is based on the massage and stimulation of reflex areas found on the feet and hands, usually focusing on the feet.

The massage sees a variety of techniques being used, but the thumb and forefinger do most of the work, smoothing and moving congestion away from reflex areas to improve health and well-being and to stimulate deep relaxation.

Mirror Images

The feet are a mirror image of the body, which can be seen in more detail on the charts featured later. The charts have developed over the years to become more comprehensive and detailed, corresponding with the progression and understanding of the craft in its reflection of the body and its parts.

To give you some idea of how the organs and body parts are positioned, imagine the toes as relating to the head, the upper portion relates to the chest and lung area, moving to the digestive area in the middle where the instep lies, with the pelvis and lower back reflexes being found in the heel; this is roughly how the body translates to the foot.

The feet are also divided up into longitudinal and horizontal zones, which enable the practitioner to pinpoint with precision the more elusive reflex areas, such as the kidney and adrenal gland reflexes. The right foot represents the right half of the body, moving from outer shoulder edge across to the inner spine reflex, while the left foot reflects the left side; each includes the organs found on the respective sides of the body.

Good Holistic Health

The way that reflexology works is quite amazing as it seems to have its effect on all aspects of the person. The physical, emotional, psychological, and spiritual self are all affected as is the body's energy system, all of which are fundamental in terms of holistic health and its principles. The body is a complex mechanism with many parts working together for the benefit of the whole being. When things are out of balance the body systems need to be encouraged to return to a harmonious state. Reflexology, as a treatment, encourages the body to return to its homeostasis, its natural state of balance. In terms of the physical aspect of the person, this therapy affects the body in a number of ways.

Firstly, there are thousands of nerve endings in the feet, which travel the length and breadth of the body. These are stimulated by the massage of the reflex areas in the feet, positively affecting the nerve function and communication in the body.

Secondly, the massage has another stimulating effect, this time concentrating on the circulatory system, improving the function of the blood and lymphatic movement. The blood and lymphatic systems have an important role in keeping the body free and clear of waste products, as well as transporting nutrients around the body; thus treatment stimulates this function, maintaining and increasing the efficacy of the circulatory systems.

Thirdly, the stimulation of the reflex areas attributed to the glands and organs, in combination with the arousal of the blood, nerve and circulatory systems, has a positive effect on the body's immune system, enhancing the innate defence mechanism's strength and responsiveness.

Benefit to Mind and Spirit

Reflexology treatment also has a positive effect on the mind and, in turn, on the spiritual aspect of the person. As the treatment progresses, the deeper the person relaxes, sometimes to a point of meditation, and it is in that place that inner healing can occur.

Breathing becomes easier and deeper, enabling oxygen to travel more efficiently through the body. The mind clears and feels lighter. Muscles relax, easing the tension normally felt in our bodies, sometimes even leading to a light, restful sleep while the treatment is

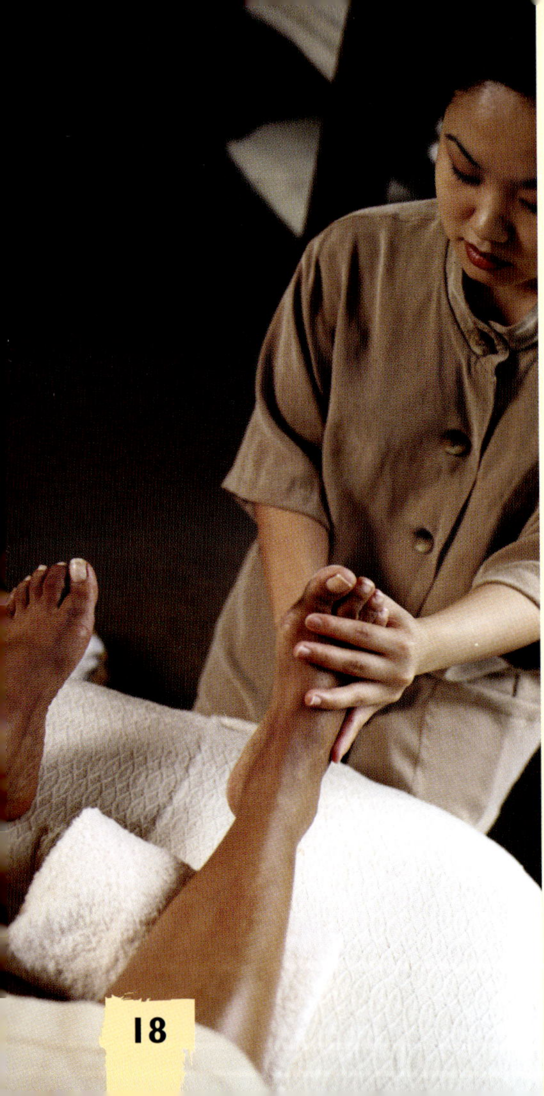

taking place. The deep relaxation eases the stresses and strains of life, clearing the clutter in the mind and helping it to regain focus – keeping that which is healthy, clearing that which is harmful. It helps you find your centre and regain communication with your inner self, something that is often neglected in our busy lives.

Facing Emotions

Another aspect of reflexology is that the time and space devoted to treatment allows us to work with, and sometimes through, some difficult emotions. All too frequently emotions are put to one side. Often we don't have the time, space or sometimes the courage to deal with this more difficult aspect of ourselves. It is important that we air our feelings and explore our emotions.

By delving into the depths of our emotions, we can discover more about our true selves and who we are; by denying our emotions, we are denying ourselves.

Energy Flow

Reflexology also has a strong connection with the Eastern principles of energy movement and energy meridians. It is believed that reflexology was developed in conjunction with the principles of acupuncture and so works with the more subtle force of Chi and its movement around the body.

Chi is an unseen force or subtle current that flows through the body, giving us life. Each person holds this energy; we obtain it through food, water and the air we breathe. The energy meridians that are seen in acupuncture show how the energy travels through the body and at what points the channels can be affected to correct the flow, dissipating any blockages that may have occurred through illness or trauma. There are twelve energy meridians that run through the body and six of these travel through the feet. Reflexology encourages the balancing of energy by opening and affecting these channels to stabilise the yin/yang and elemental equilibrium.

Reflexology is a multifaceted treatment as it works from a holistic perspective, whilst also encouraging the body to rid itself of toxins and impurities. It can normalise the function of glands, organs and hormones, ease away the tension that gathers in the mind and body, explore our emotional being and balance the energy within us while gently persuading a return to homeostasis. It is a very valuable tool to combat stress and tension, reinstating balance.

Metaphysical Link

The link between the mind and the body has become a widely publicised area of relevance to a person's state of health and well-being. Its prominence has grown over the last twenty years or so, seeing the mind and emotions as having much more of an effect on the body than had previously been recognised.

When giving or receiving a treatment such as reflexology, it is important to bear in mind the relevance of emotions, thoughts, life changes and past trauma when looking at a person's state of health. Any conditions, illnesses and disease that they may carry, as a state of disease within an individual however it may arise, can indicate a great deal about a person's life and background.

Quite often, when asking about the situation surrounding an accident or illness in a person's past, they can identify a traumatic or emotional event which was prominent at or around the same time. The body has the ability to communicate physically what is troubling it emotionally, psychologically, and spiritually.

Under Pressure

We all know the link between ill-health and stress. The constant pressure of work and life can build and contribute to a lowered immune response and other medical conditions. But do we pay close enough attention to the messages that our bodies give us?

Mind, Body and Spirit

We experience reactions between the mind, body, and emotions almost constantly in our everyday life. These reactions can manifest themselves with sensations of 'butterflies' in the stomach when we are nervous or anxious, or the instantaneous 'gut' reaction when we meet someone we're not sure of, as well as the well-chronicled experience when love is felt and acknowledged. These just highlight the link that exists between mind, spirit and body. As you delve deeper into states of being and the physical reaction or response to them, you begin to comprehend the relationship between these parts.

Thousands of chemical messages are sent throughout the body every minute of the day. There is evidence to suggest that our moods, emotions and state of being can affect the way that these are sent and received. The nerves receiving messages must also be affected in the same way. If, for instance, there is an area of tension in the body, this challenges the effectiveness of the messages being received or carried.

Emotions, illness, and trauma also influence the way our body works, affecting our state of health, interrupting energy pathways, and disturbing the body's natural rhythms and cycles. Reflexology treatment often finds that a past emotive experience fixes itself somewhere within the body until its release can be properly managed, the experience acknowledged, and its relevance understood and put to rest.

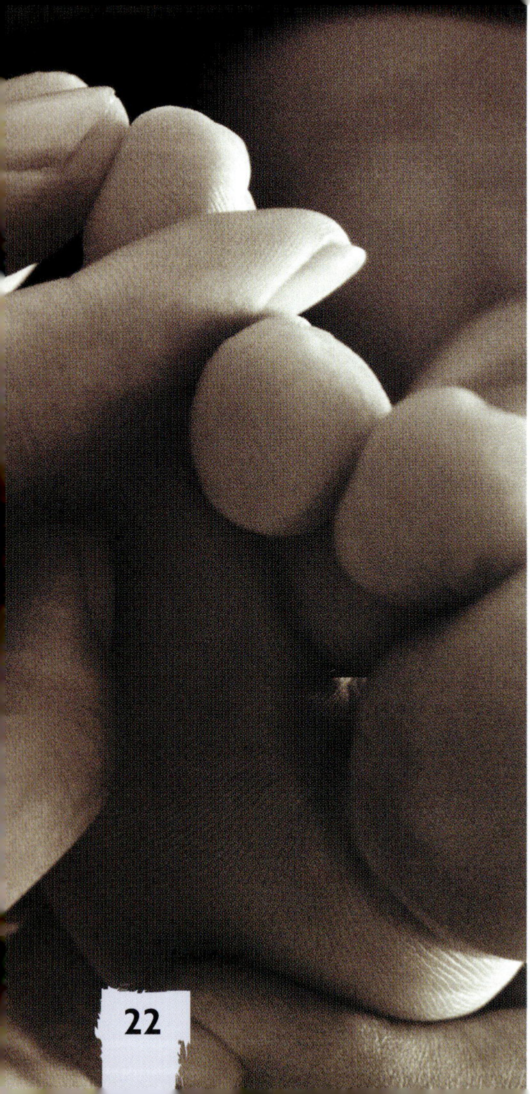

Who CAN HAVE treatment?

Reflexology is good for people of all ages and may be beneficial for ailments and illnesses, although there are some conditions that the practitioner has to be aware of to be able to adapt the treatment accordingly.

The treatment of certain illnesses and conditions should be avoided by the amateur and require the attention of a fully qualified and experienced practitioner.

The most important tool that any practitioner has at their disposal when encountering any situation they may be unsure of is intuition. If it feels like a treatment should be altered or adapted, the practitioner will change the routine according to their own inner voice.

A therapy for all ages

Babies and children require shorter treatment time as they have a shorter span of concentration and smaller feet. The treatment for babies generally focuses on soothing and relaxing, using gentle, sweeping massage strokes. Children can handle a shorter treatment than that of an adult, and one that is adapted according to their needs.

WARNING

People suffering from epilepsy, diabetes or any other medical condition or disease should only be treated by a professional reflexologist after consultation with a doctor.

Pregnant women will, similarly, need to consult a professional.

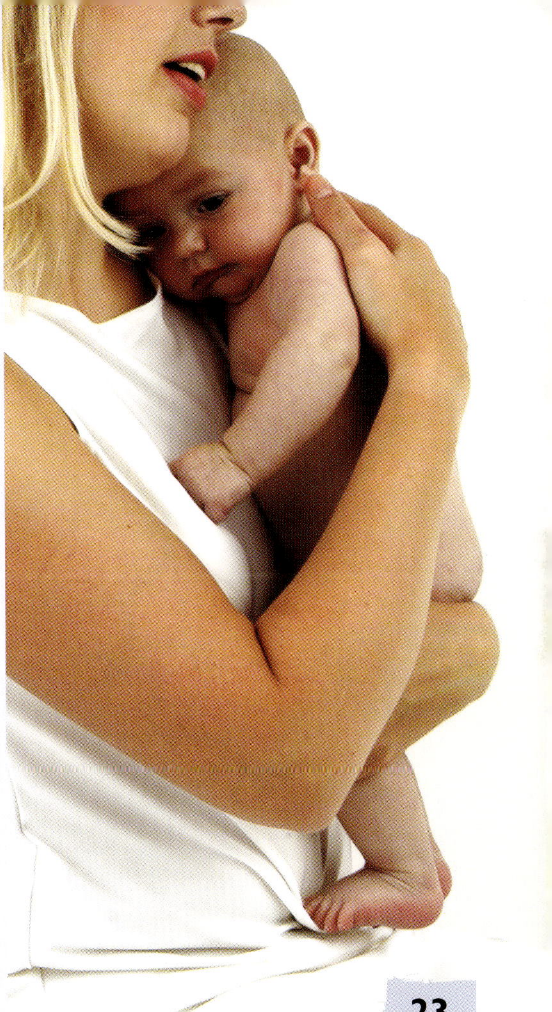

Care should be taken when treating the elderly as their skin is generally much thinner, making the patient more sensitive to pressure. Treatments require adaptation and extra consideration from the practitioner.

Medical Matters

Medical conditions such as pregnancy, diabetes, epilepsy, unstable blood pressure and heart conditions, thrombosis and cancer require the experience of a qualified reflexologist who may in turn need to gain consent for treatment from a medical practitioner. These conditions do not necessarily prevent a person from receiving treatment but require greater awareness and caution from the practitioner.

Reflexology treatment has been of benefit to many. It has helped to alleviate pain, tension and symptoms of illness and can also offer some improvement to certain medical conditions.

Stress and tension obviously head the list of the most successfully treated conditions, but are joined by a whole host of other ailments such as migraines, hormonal imbalances, nervous conditions, muscular tension and pain, palliative care, pre- and postnatal care, arthritis and rheumatism. Each individual has their own personal experience and reaction to treatment, which is affected by the emotional and physical history of the person. The subjective nature of the treatment means that results are never certain but there is generally an overall positive reaction or response.

Finding a practitioner

Many people like to go to someone who has been recommended to them by a friend and 'word of mouth' is the most popular way of finding a suitable practitioner. It can often be the most effective, too.

Finding the right practitioner for you is very important, as the success of a treatment is also based on your interaction with the practitioner.

Some people find that they like the treatment but don't 'click' with the therapist. Should this happen, don't give up on the treatment if you think it may work for you. Instead find an alternative practitioner either by recommendation, via various organisations or local complementary health centres.

Every practitioner has a different style of working and some may not suit certain people, so make it your quest to find the right person for you.

Another good way of finding a practitioner is to keep an eye open for health and healing fairs in your area where you may be able to experience a taster treatment for a reduced price. This will give you an opportunity to meet and decide on a practitioner to suit you.

Relaxed Environment

The location of treatment is sometimes an influencing factor when choosing a therapist, as it is important to feel comfortable and relaxed when receiving treatment. You will probably find that a lot of therapists practise from a centre, whilst others set aside a treatment room in their home. There are also those who make home visits for people who are unable to travel for any reason. These are all considerations when finding a practitioner; remember to go with what feels right for you.

What to EXPECT

When visiting someone or doing anything for the first time, it is always best to have some idea of what to expect before it actually happens. This chapter gives some detail on what happens when you visit a reflexologist and what you may have to be aware of afterwards.

All reflexologists have different ways of working but there are a few common features of most practices.

On your first visit, the therapist will take a case history, asking questions about aspects of your life from which they can gain a clearer picture of who you are, and what areas of the feet may need more attention during the treatment. The questions usually cover your medical and emotional history, diet and other aspects of life.

The duration of the treatment itself can vary as all reflexologists work at their own pace, but generally it takes from 45 minutes to an hour to complete a session. The elderly and children sometimes require a shorter treatment, but generally the practitioner relies on their own intuition for guidance in such circumstances.

During treatment your body may have certain immediate reactions to the stimulus.

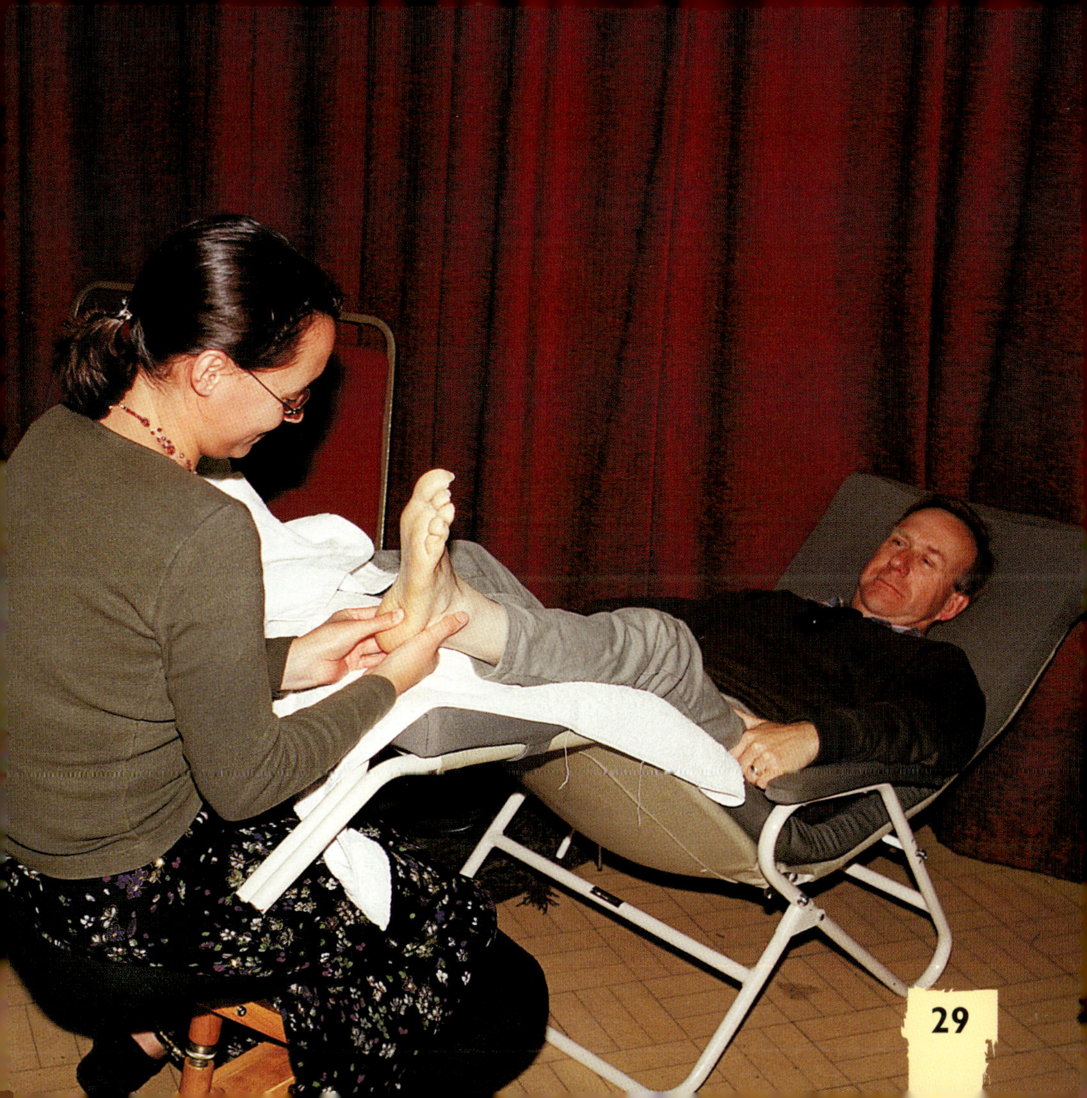

The following list covers the most common responses.

* Usually, your body and breathing relaxes, easing away tension. However, because it is a new situation and you are unsure what to expect, this may not occur as soon as you had anticipated.

* You may experience a tingling sensation, which runs through the body as the energy flow of the nervous system improves, occasionally being felt in the area being worked on.

* Sometimes the stomach starts growling as the tension releases and it is then able to move things more freely.

* Your body temperature can sometimes fluctuate as the energy and toxins move through the body. Don't be afraid to pick up a blanket!

* Emotions that have been suppressed, or prevalent in the time leading up to treatment can sometimes reveal themselves. Don't be fearful of this event, it happens infrequently but is usually necessary as part of the healing process. Try not to resist it, release is the best remedy.

* Some pain may be felt during treatment over reflex areas that hold tension or relate to a condition or problem area that you may be aware of. The tenderness does ease as the tension or area is released and the therapist will work according to your needs. Generally, tenderness and congestion signal a toxin build-up, muscle tension, or an emotional issue caught up in the body, and sometimes an energy blockage or imbalance – working on these areas can facilitate the healing process and any discomfort should ease.

* People can, and do, fall asleep during treatment. Don't worry if sleep overpowers you, the treatment is all about healing and bringing yourself back to centre. Sometimes sleep is what the body needs and is where the healing can begin.

* When the treatment has finished you may feel disorientated. You should try to remain seated until you feel more alert and coherent. Allowing a few minutes to regain your senses is even more important if you need to drive home after the session.

* After treatment, as the toxins try to move out of the body, you may feel a few side effects. The best thing to do after treatment is to drink plenty of water. The water will help the body flush out the toxins that the session has stimulated. The movement of water will also hydrate the body and its organs, and help contribute to the energy boost felt later.

Side effects

The most common side effects felt after treatment are listed below but do remember that they are a positive experience as it means that the treatment has had an effect and is trying to return the body to a balanced state.

* Headache and lethargy are the most common side effects. These indicate that the body is trying to clear itself of toxins and impurities and are most easily remedied by drinking lots of water.

* Visiting the toilet more often signals the release of impurities and waste, clearing a sluggish digestive system.

* A release of emotions can occur and it is best to let them go and work with them as they often trigger a healing experience.

* If you are harbouring a cold germ or a virus, the treatment can sometimes bring the illness out, as its aim is to bring balance to the body, ridding the body of any impurity.
* It helps promote a deeper sleep after treatment.
* If treating a specific condition, the symptoms may appear to get worse during the 24 hours after treatment, which then lift and, in most cases, disappear.

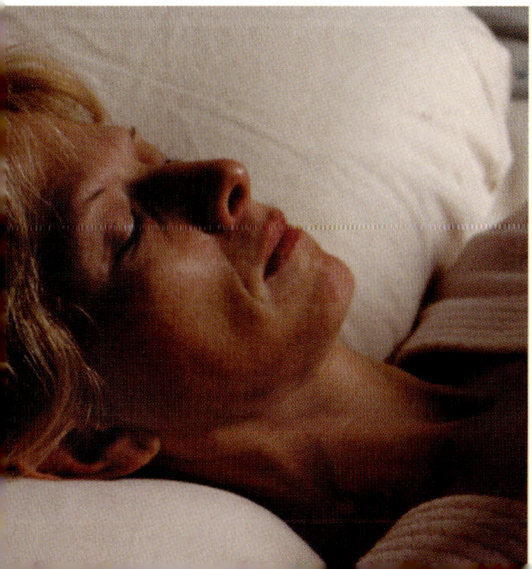

These things don't always happen with treatment, everybody is different and each treatment varies, but they are an indication of the possibilities.

Any effect of treatment, even negative, is a sign that it has worked, and most side effects pass after about 24 hours. Sometimes the treatment is very subtle and so some side effects may not be felt at all but usually most people experience the 'floaty', relaxed feeling that a reflexology session gives you.

Remember to pay attention to your body during and after treatment, as it is almost always trying to tell you something, even if it is only telling you that you need to drink some more water!

Treating YOURSELF

Reflexology is a wonderful therapy to give and receive; it strengthens relationships and friendships, bringing people closer together, whilst also having a positive effect on both the mind and body.

The relaxation this therapy promotes is amazing, as it is able to improve one's state of health and being at the same time. It is just as relaxing to give as it is to receive. The interaction of energies and having such a positive effect on someone contribute to a shared feeling of warmth and well-being.

Rescue Routines

The rescue routines featured within this book are ideal to treat those around you who may be suffering with the ailments listed.

They are basic guides to help others and if you enjoy the experience of treating others and wish to take it further, then look for a certificated course in your area that will give you the knowledge, support and guidance a reflexology practitioner needs to treat the general public.

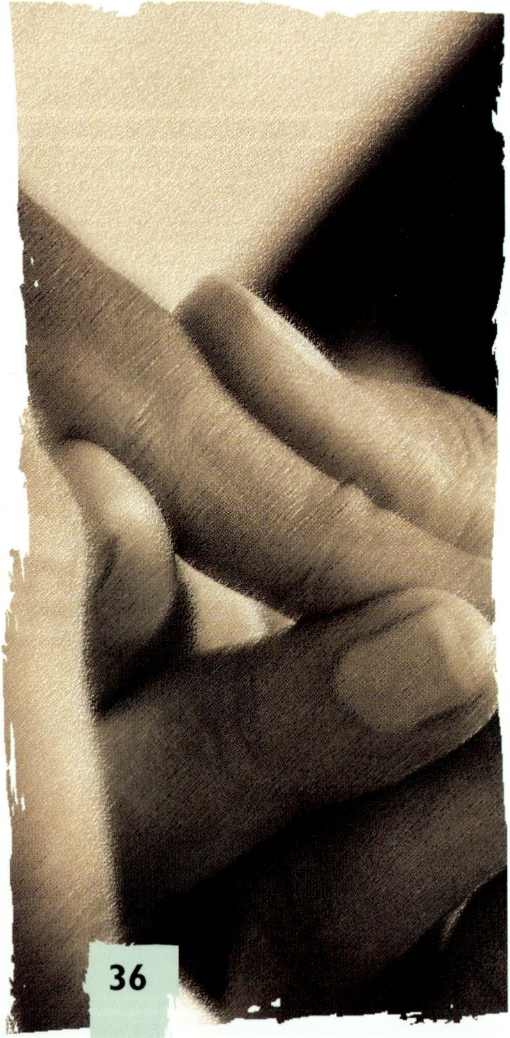

Hand Reflexology

On some occasions, it may be necessary to treat the hands rather than the feet due to personal preference or an actual physical problem such as broken bones, a sprained ankle, surgery or a wound on the foot.

Hand reflexology gives a slightly different response than when treating the feet, the results being of a more spiritual and psychological nature, yet still having a physical effect upon the person.

It is more of a connective treatment between the giver and receiver. The hands generally express more about the person, communicating their needs and their response to others and so can help strengthen and enhance bonds within the family environment. Treatment of the hands also has a greater capacity to soothe and calm the receiver.

Physical Aspect

Hand reflexology is a great method for helping any physical aspect directly and discreetly when in need of relief from any physical pain or feeling when 'out of balance'. This gives you, the individual, the ability to try to steady yourself or others in times of need.

Practically, when following the guidelines in this book for the specific routines, you will need to alter some of the techniques since the physicality of every person's hand is different, as are the positions of the reflexes. The enclosed hand chart details the locations and layout of the reflexes and will need to be closely referred to when trying to apply the routines.

Practising

When practising hand reflexology it is best for the giver and receiver to sit side by side at a slight angle so that a pillow or cushion perched across both laps can comfortably support the receiver's hands.

In stimulating the reflexes on the hands, a different use of technique is needed. Feet reflexology mainly employs the 'caterpillar walking' routine (p. 57), but on the hands that is only used when working the sinus areas, the spine reflexes, the lymphatic area on the dorsal aspect and when stimulating the large intestine reflex. The fleshiness of the palms requires a small circular movement of the thumb travelling over the entirety of the reflex. The same hooking technique is used for the pituitary and ileo-cecal valve reflexes on the hands as it is for the feet, with the kidney/adrenal reflex possibly requiring the hooking technique (depending on the size of the hands and the accessibility of the reflex.)

Spiritual Aspect

Hand reflexology is a very gentle treatment, as the fingers represent the head and its related parts. The proportional dominance of the fingers to the hand means that therapy relates more to the healing and balancing of the mind and the spiritual aspect of the person. The effects more commonly experienced after this treatment usually relate to a change of consciousness, moving towards a more positive psychological state together with increased spiritual awareness of oneself and one's place in the world.

Hand treatment

To work the larger reflex areas on the palm of the hand, use your thumb to make small, circular movements across the reflex, working from the medial to lateral side (a).

a

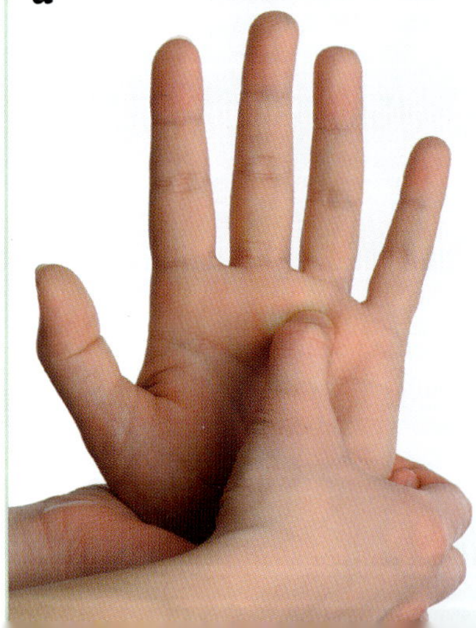

Use your thumb to caterpillar walk along the spine reflex while supporting the vulnerable thumb with the forefinger of the same hand (b).

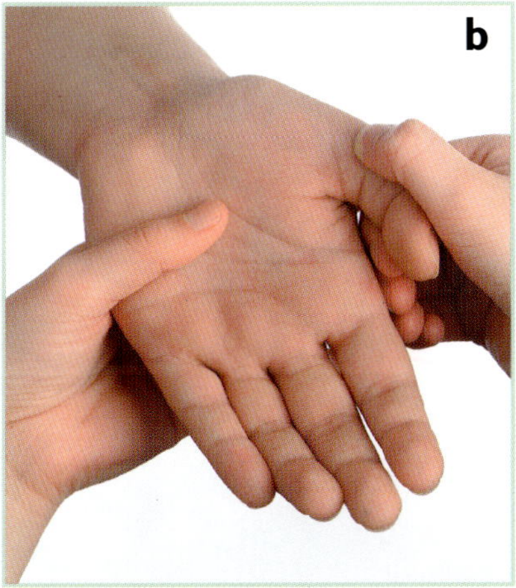

The push/squeeze technique can also be used on the hand, being just as relaxing as when used on the foot. With the flat of the fist resting on the upper part of the palm, push into the hand, release, and then reply with a gentle squeeze using the other hand (c).

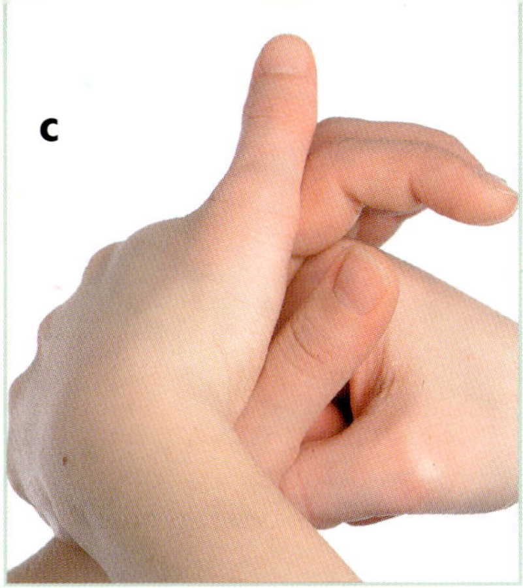

Caterpillar walking between the phalanges on the back of the hand can aid lymphatic drainage and clearing. An area to be gently worked on the elderly (d).

Preparation

Before reflexology treatment commences, it is always a good idea to look at making the environment and experience as relaxing and nurturing as possible.

There are several factors to the experience that can improve the treatment; the environment has to be quiet and free from distractions before you begin to promote relaxation.

A comfortable position is needed for both people involved in the treatment. Ensure you have ascertained any specific medical requirements or any conditions that may affect treatment. Finally, make sure the feet themselves are fully prepared for treatment.

To prepare a relaxing environment, consider taking the phone off the hook and make sure that there will be no interruptions so that the treatment can be as relaxing as possible. Play some soothing music in the background, perhaps even light a few candles and have some essential oils vaporising in order to help create the right ambience.

Make sure the position of each person involved in the treatment is as comfortable as possible. Accommodate for the possibility of deep relaxation and sleep for the person receiving treatment. It is best not to twist and contort your body if giving treatment as it should be relaxing for both parties.

A good habit to get into before each treatment is to pamper the feet. This aids relaxation and signifies the beginning of quality time for the recipient.

A foot soak helps soften any hard skin, particularly if you include oil or bath salts in the water. As the skin softens it is the ideal opportunity to work away at accumulation of hard skin with a pumice stone or foot file. Take care not to make the feet sore with any over-zealous attempts.

After a soothing soak, your feet should feel gorgeous. To help maintain the feeling and keep hard skin and dryness

at bay, a good moisturiser will improve the condition of the foot. If you don't have access to a foot spa, a small wooden massager is good for stimulating the reflexes further and the circulation in general.

If time doesn't allow for a foot soak, use a couple of wipes to cleanse the feet. Use lotion or foot powder to help the massage and motion of the fingers over the feet during treatment.

It is always a good idea to have some drinking water available for both parties. For the recipient, water encourages the body to clear itself of toxins and impurities as well as helping moisten a dry throat which can often occur during treatment.

A more practical consideration is the length of the nails of the person giving the treatment. It can be very uncomfortable having a nail delving into the foot when working a specific reflex.

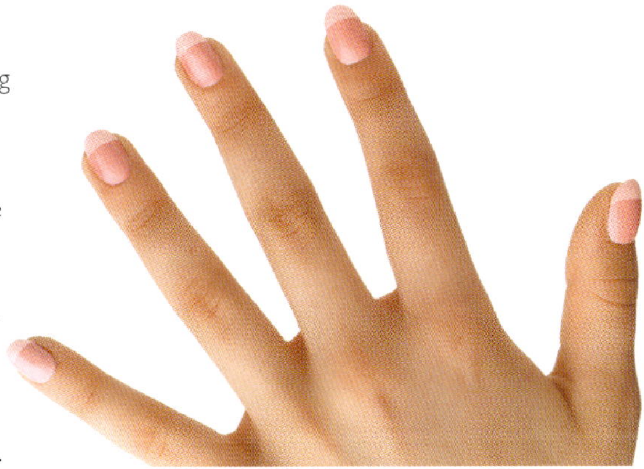

Reflexology treatment is a nurturing, healing experience, that promotes realisation and transformation through positive action. The conditions under which the treatment takes place can be very influential in terms of allowing the person receiving treatment to open up and allow the experience to permeate their being and develop their sense of self.

What to look for on the feet

A good way to begin treatment is to notice the nuances and characteristics of the feet.

All feet are different and have varying shapes due to bone structure and how we carry ourselves in everyday life; skin texture, colour and shape can tell us a great deal about a person before the treatment has commenced, not only on a physical level but also metaphysically.

Conditions such as bunions, hammer toes, fallen arches, webbed toes, corns, and calluses can be attributed to being inherited from parents, or as a result of improper care of the feet by wearing the wrong shoes. However, some conditions of the feet and ankles may also be attributed to lower back problems, while others require a strong need to recognise the metaphysical link in relation to the characteristics of the feet.

The texture of the skin is important; any hard skin indicates resistance in an area of life, or a build-up of physical tension as a result of stress. Similarly, rough skin indicates a period of strain in the recipient's life. Flaky skin can indicate a process of change or that someone, or something, is having a deep effect on the person.

The colours of the feet are also very important. A deep red colour can signify a build-up of emotion and a busy lifestyle; while a pale, white-coloured foot

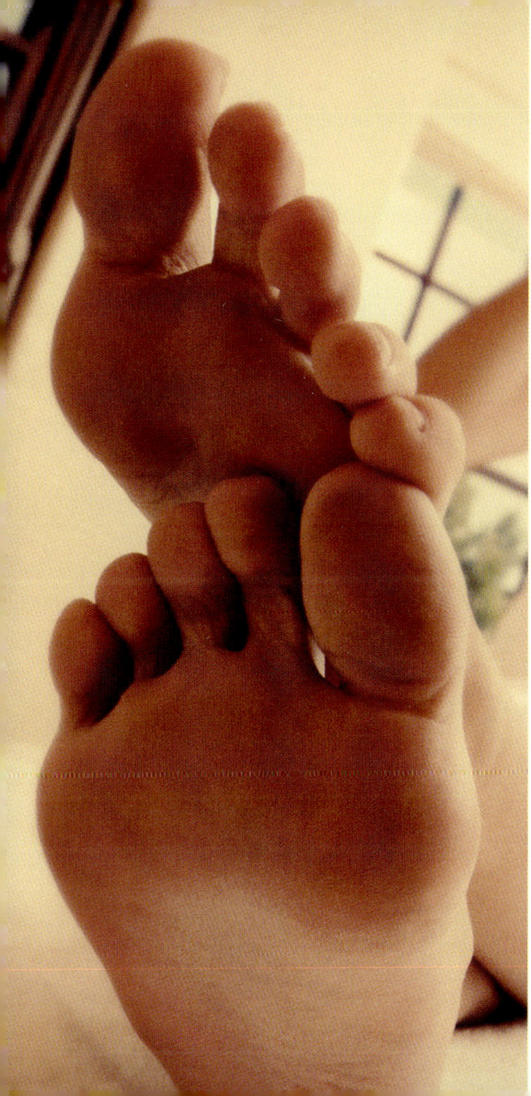

indicates a tired, emotionally drained person. Yellowish feet reveal a need for cleansing the body, signalling an accumulation of toxins or a feeling of anger and resentment. Flashes of purple or black in specific areas, such as the head, pancreas and/or the thymus, point to intense emotional activity, particularly feelings of grief and loss.

Areas of swelling over certain reflexes can reflect a build-up of a significant emotion particular to the specific reflex. Swelling may also point to an accumulation of muscular tension, or in cases of arthritis, highlight the joints that are most affected by the condition.

Tenderness felt on the foot during treatment often indicates an area where tension or toxins have gathered and need to be dissipated. It can also indicate blocked energy, underlying or

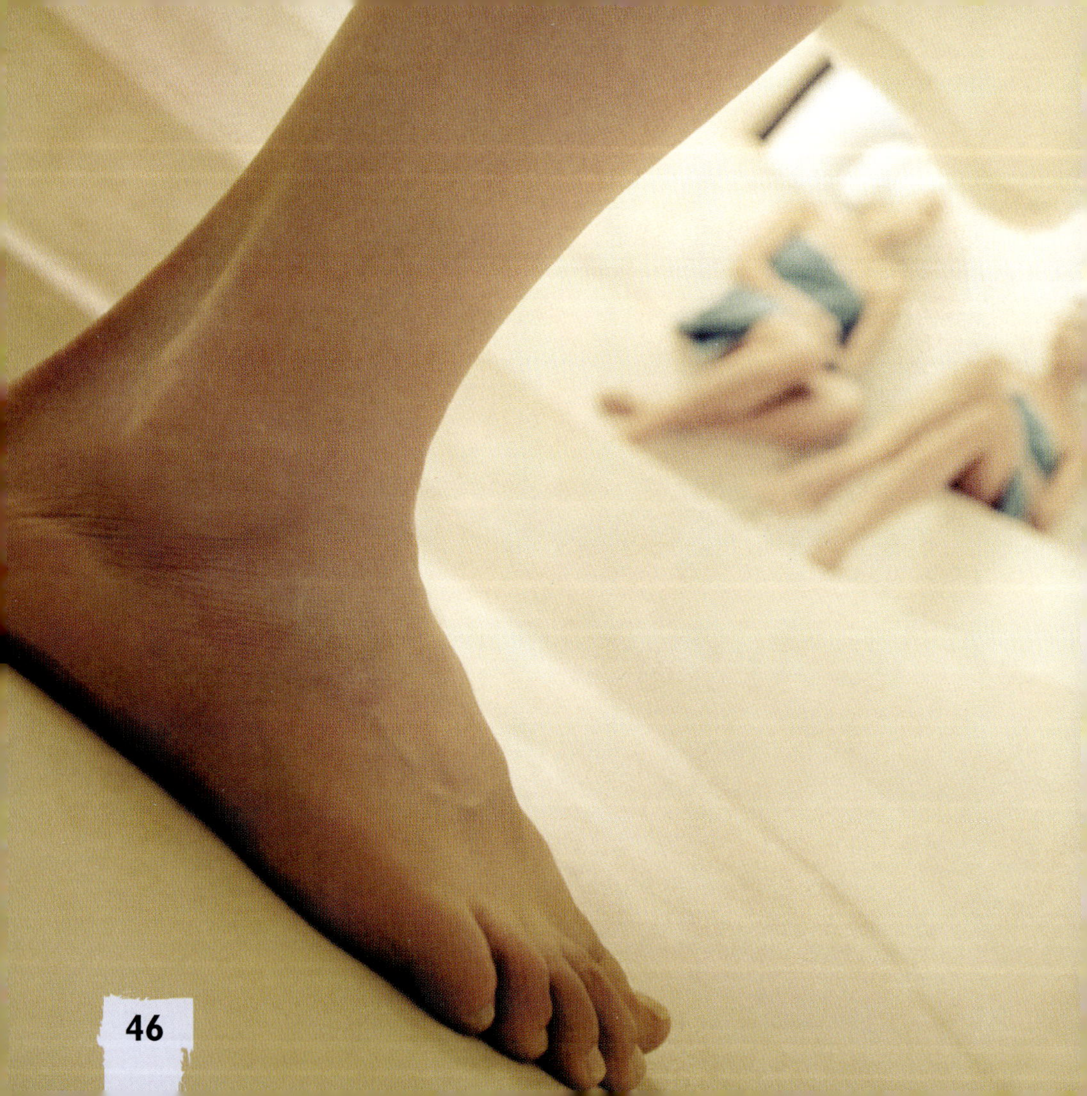

unresolved emotions or issues, and the body's weaker areas. The tenderness often dissipates as the area is worked upon.

Detecting underlying congestion on the reflexes of the hands or feet is a skill that takes time to master, but practice will increase your sensitivity.

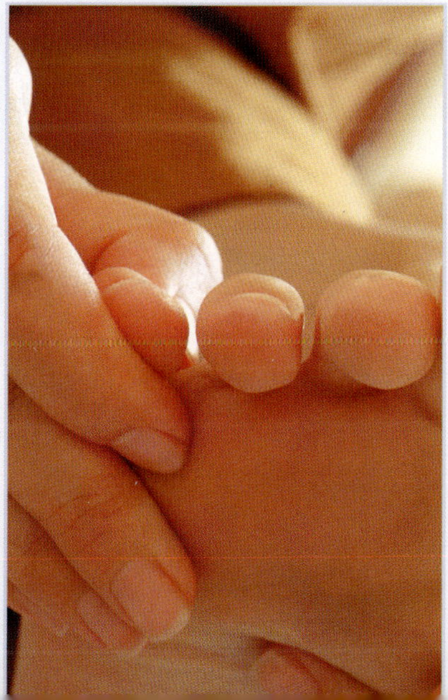

The congestion felt on, or around, the reflexes can generally be described as being like grains of sand but it can take the form of a hard mass. Slight swellings may also be felt, and in time you can begin to feel intuitively when there may be tenderness even when there is no physical sign of congestion.

Studying the feet and understanding their nuances is an art in itself and takes time to develop, but it is intriguing that just by looking on the surface, we can notice more of the intricacies of a person and begin to understand them.

Until you are proficient in reflexology you will need to refer constantly to foot and hand charts to direct you to the relevant reflex points.

These charts follow in the next few pages and should be studied closely before beginning any treatment.

Right Foot – Plantar Aspect

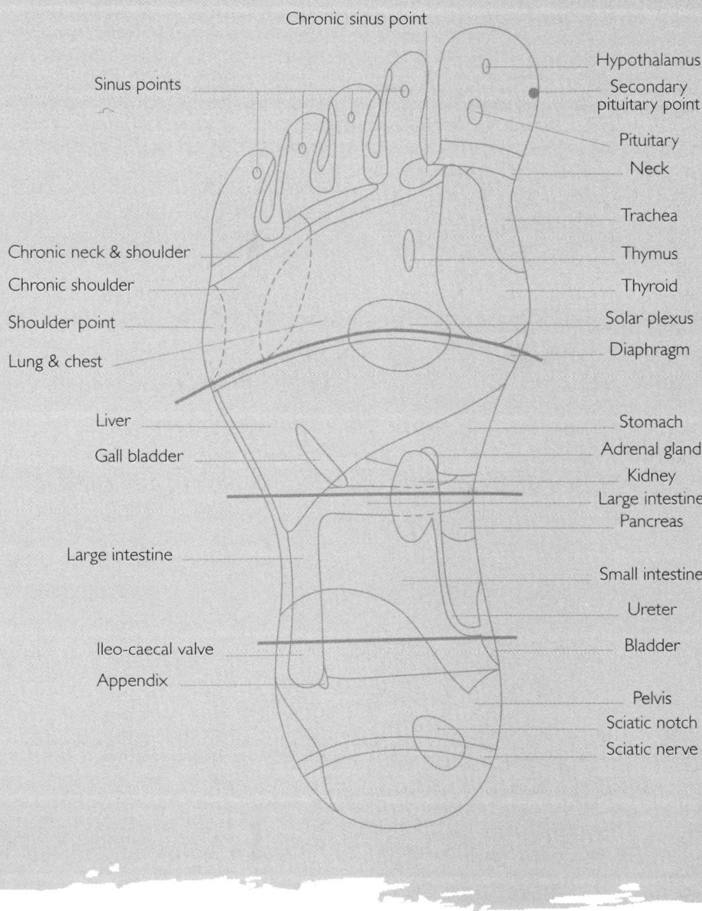

Left Foot – Plantar Aspect

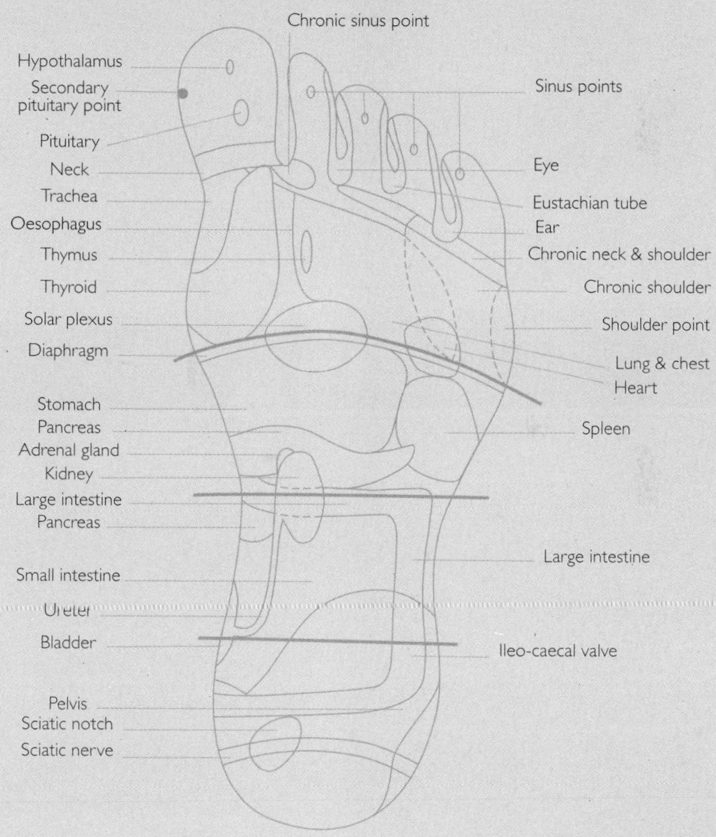

Dorsal Aspect

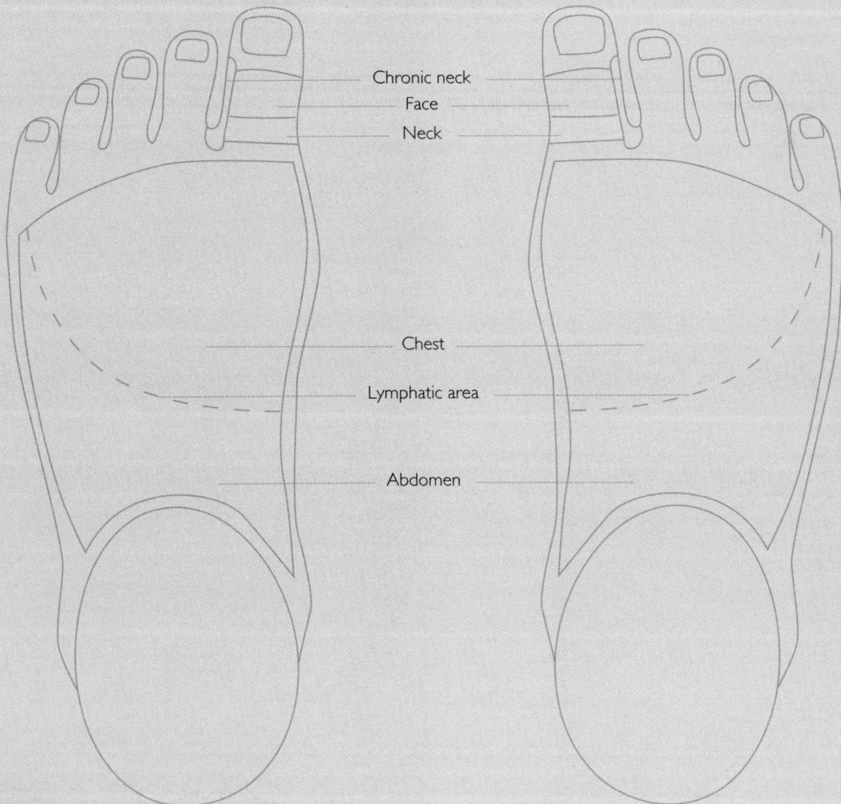

Medial Aspect

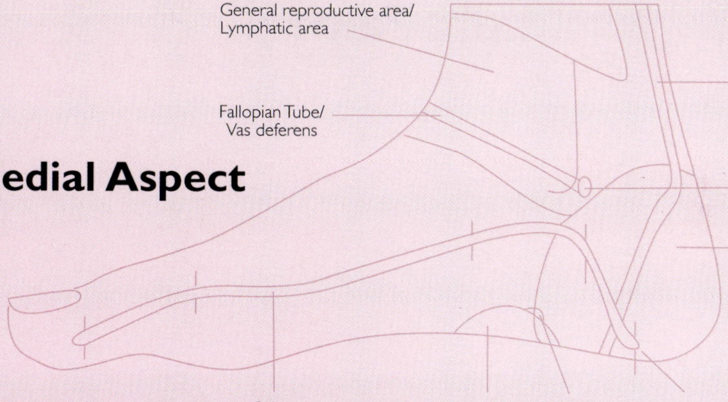

Lateral Aspect

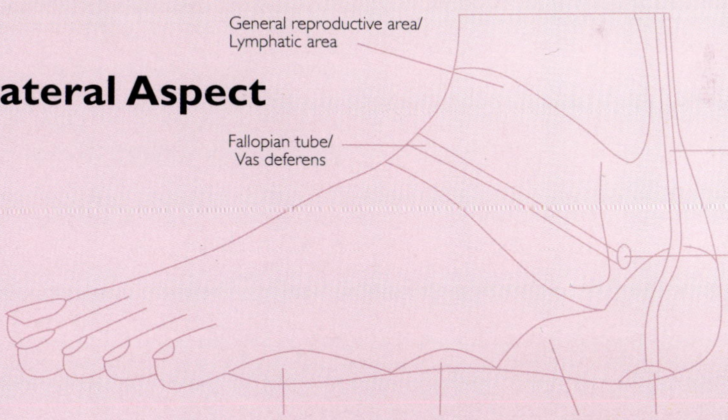

Left Palm

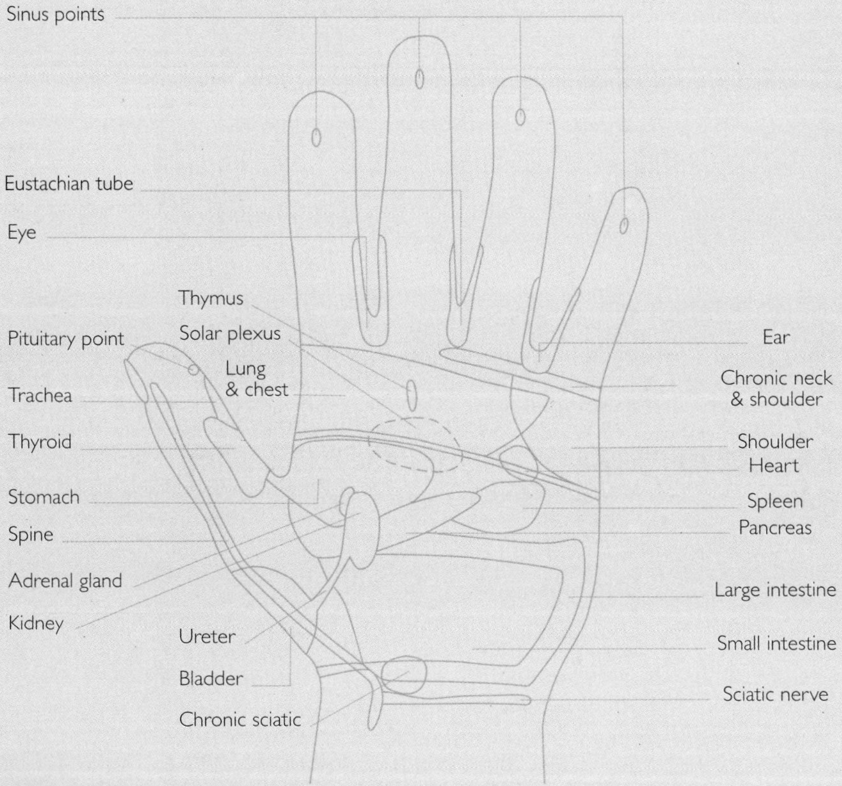
Sinus points
Eustachian tube
Eye
Thymus
Solar plexus
Pituitary point
Lung
& chest
Trachea
Thyroid
Stomach
Spine
Adrenal gland
Kidney
Ureter
Bladder
Chronic sciatic
Ear
Chronic neck
& shoulder
Shoulder
Heart
Spleen
Pancreas
Large intestine
Small intestine
Sciatic nerve

Right Palm

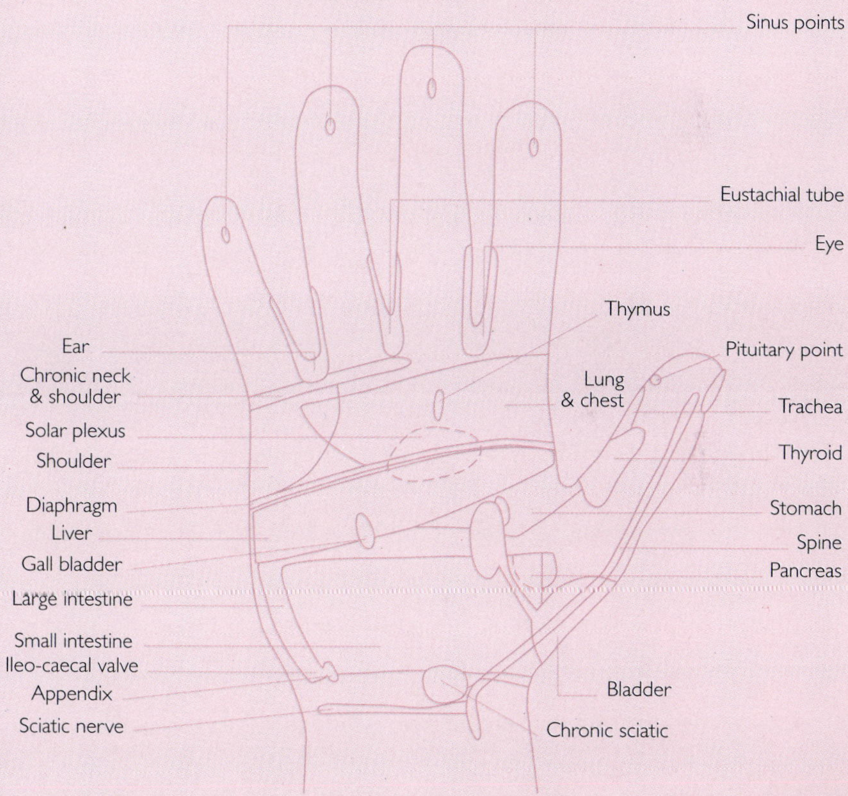

Sinus points
Eustachial tube
Eye
Thymus
Ear
Chronic neck
& shoulder
Pituitary point
Lung
& chest
Trachea
Solar plexus
Shoulder
Thyroid
Diaphragm
Stomach
Liver
Spine
Gall bladder
Pancreas
Large intestine
Small intestine
Ileo-caecal valve
Bladder
Appendix
Sciatic nerve
Chronic sciatic

Left Dorsal Aspect

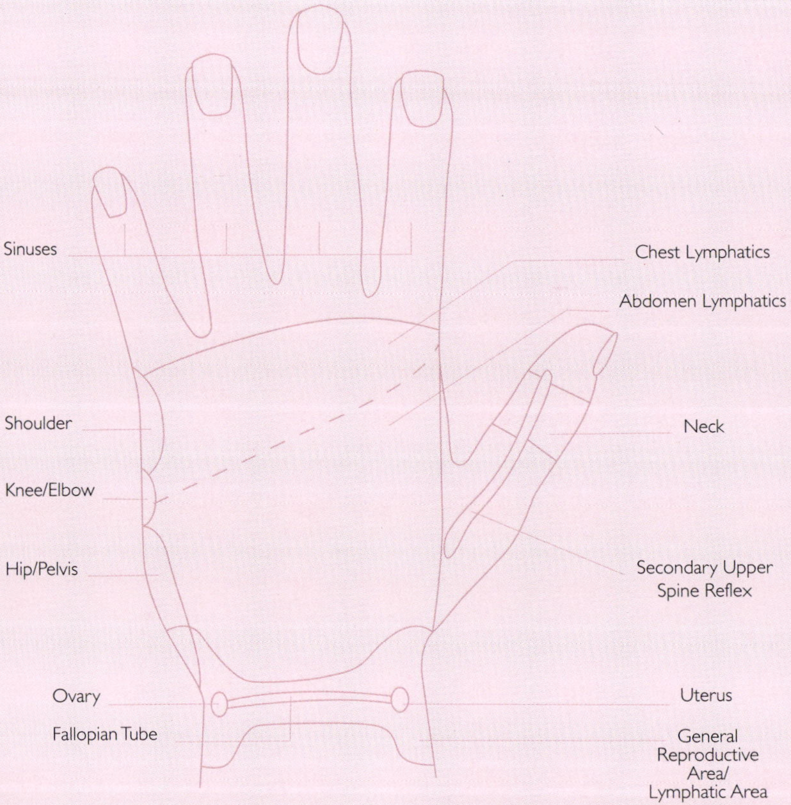

Right Dorsal Aspect

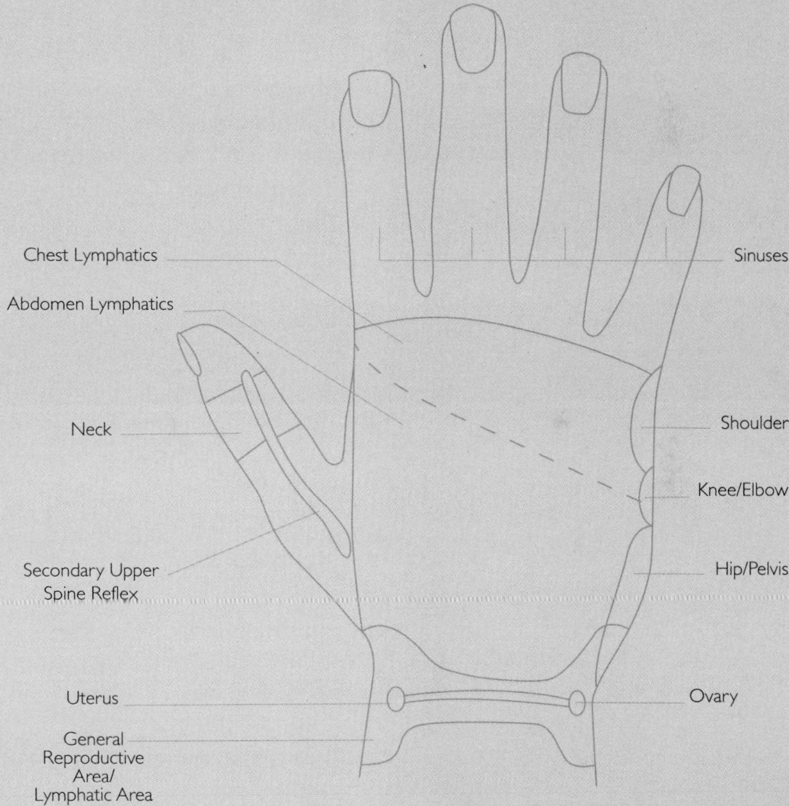

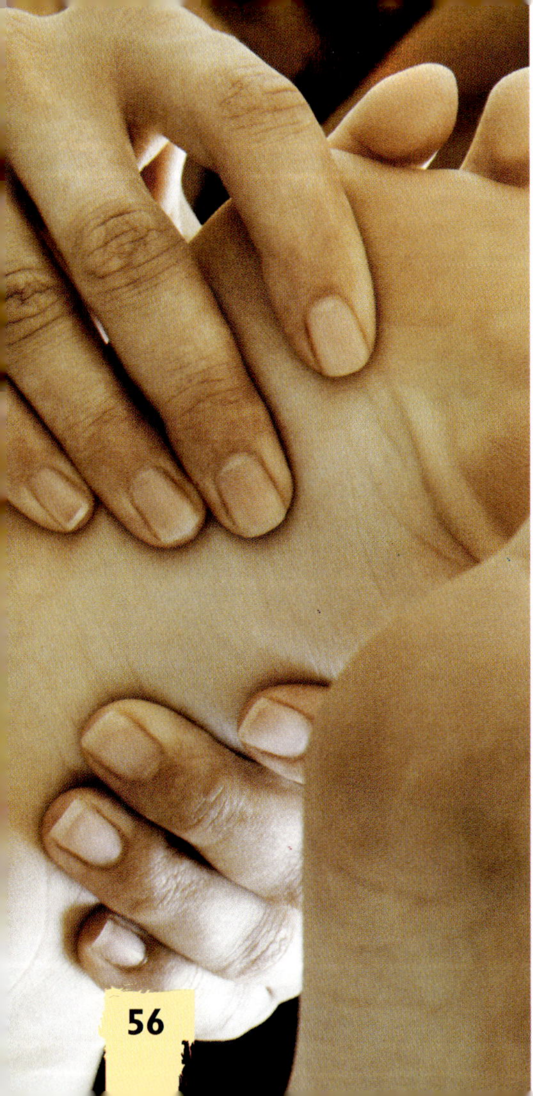

Techniques

This chapter will show you the techniques needed for working the reflexes on the feet and hands.

The sensitivity for feeling any congestion over the reflexes builds over time, so don't worry if this still isn't very highly attuned to start with. For all of these techniques, it is best to practise on yourself to begin with, so you begin to feel the amount of pressure needed and become more aware of the congestion that may be felt.

When working the feet, it is best to concentrate on working one foot at a time, moving onto the next foot when the routine has been completed. It is generally best to treat the right foot before moving onto the left. This helps continuity and development of the treatment and gives better results.

'caterpillar walking'

The most common finger and thumb technique used is that of 'caterpillar walking'.

Holding the first joint of the thumb or finger(s) at an angle, move along the surface area by moving in small steps, mimicking the movement of a caterpillar, while maintaining a steady and even pressure.

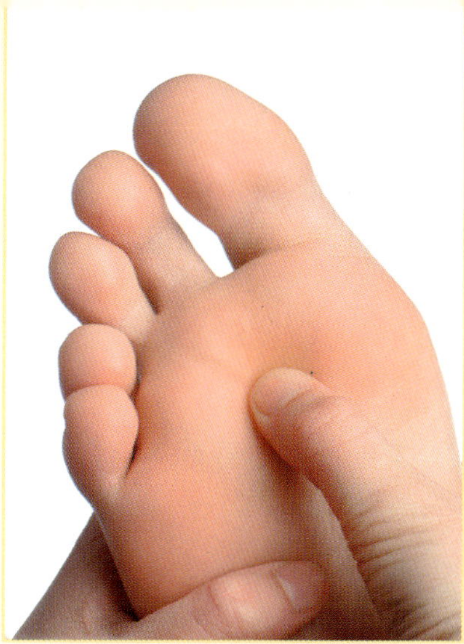

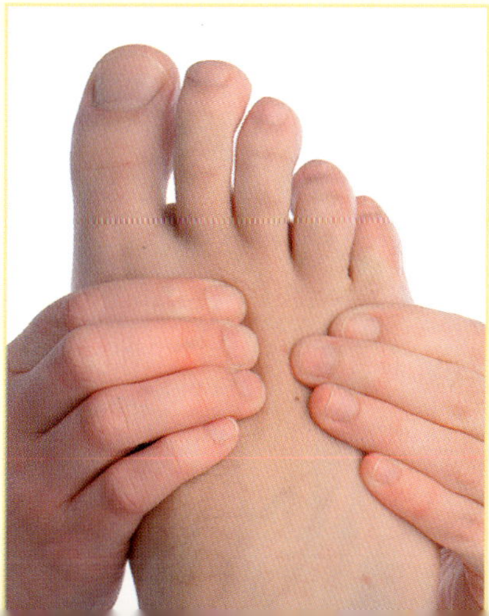

This technique is also known as thumb- or finger-walking. For the chest and abdominal area on the top of the foot (dorsal), multi-finger walking is required to cover the surface area evenly and effectively.

‘hooking’

In order to stimulate two areas of the feet, namely the pituitary gland and the ileo-caecal valve, the ‘hooking’ movement is required.

This is achieved by holding the thumb at an angle, pushing down on the small reflex and pulling out again in one smooth motion without releasing the pressure. It can be quite an intense movement so be aware of the person’s reaction when using this technique.

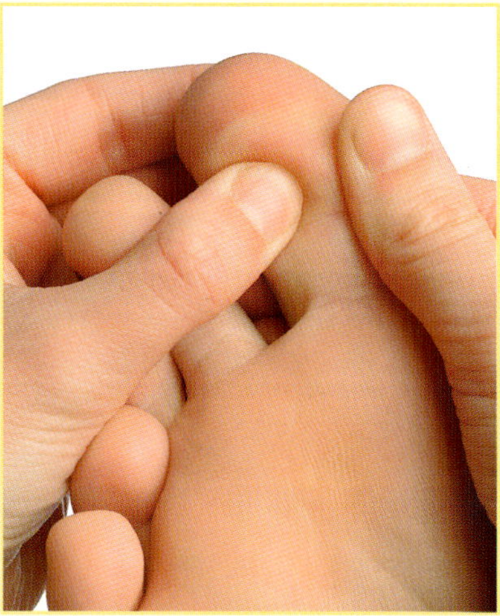

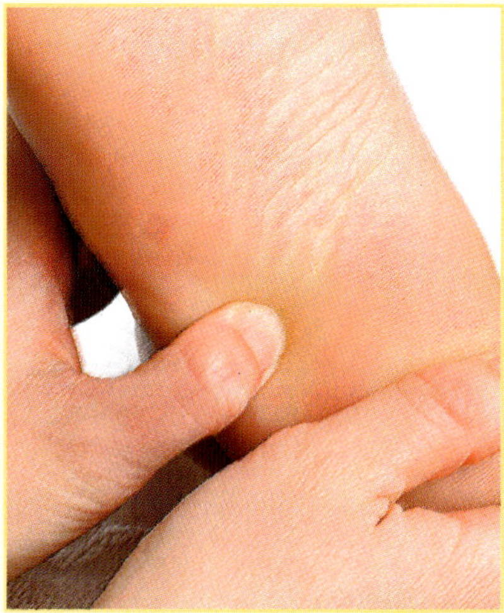

‘pressure focus’

Occasionally, there will be the need to focus on a specific point to clear energy or try to encourage the release of areas of congestion.

This can be achieved by two methods. One is by rotating on the point for release with one finger. The other is by maintaining a steady pressure, hooking in on the reflex and releasing after a shift is felt, or when the pressure or tenderness felt by the recipient becomes too intense.

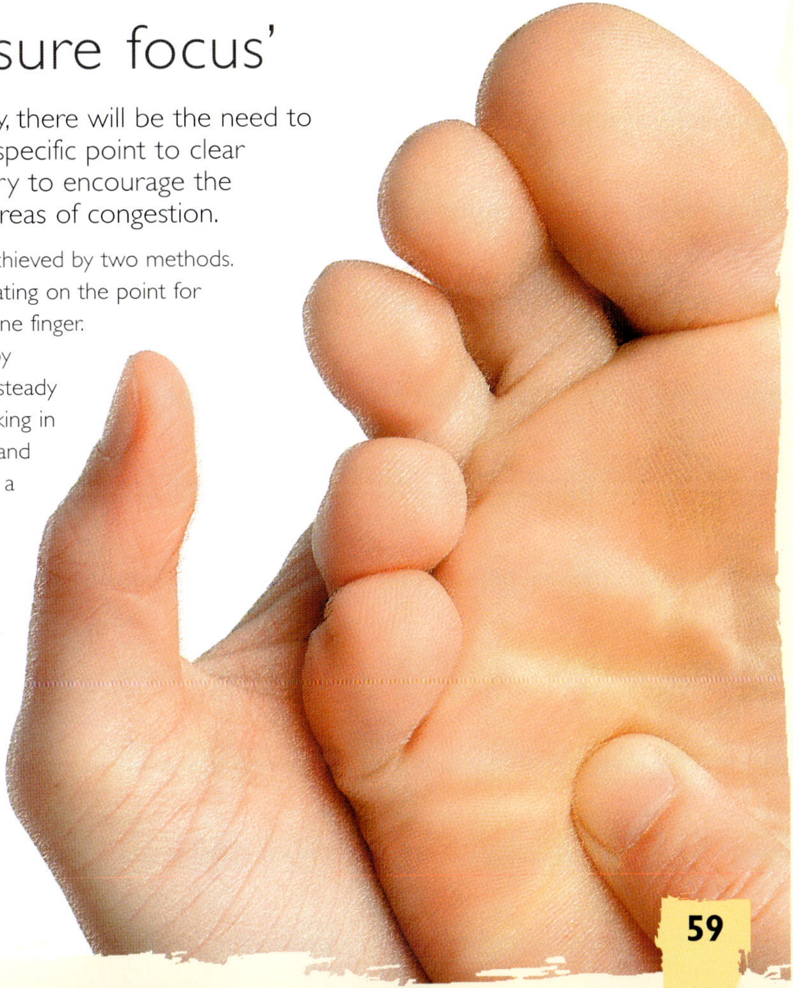

'solar plexus hold'

An important technique for beginning and ending the treatment is the 'solar plexus hold' as it soothes and calms while allowing the energies to flow freely between the two people involved in the treatment.

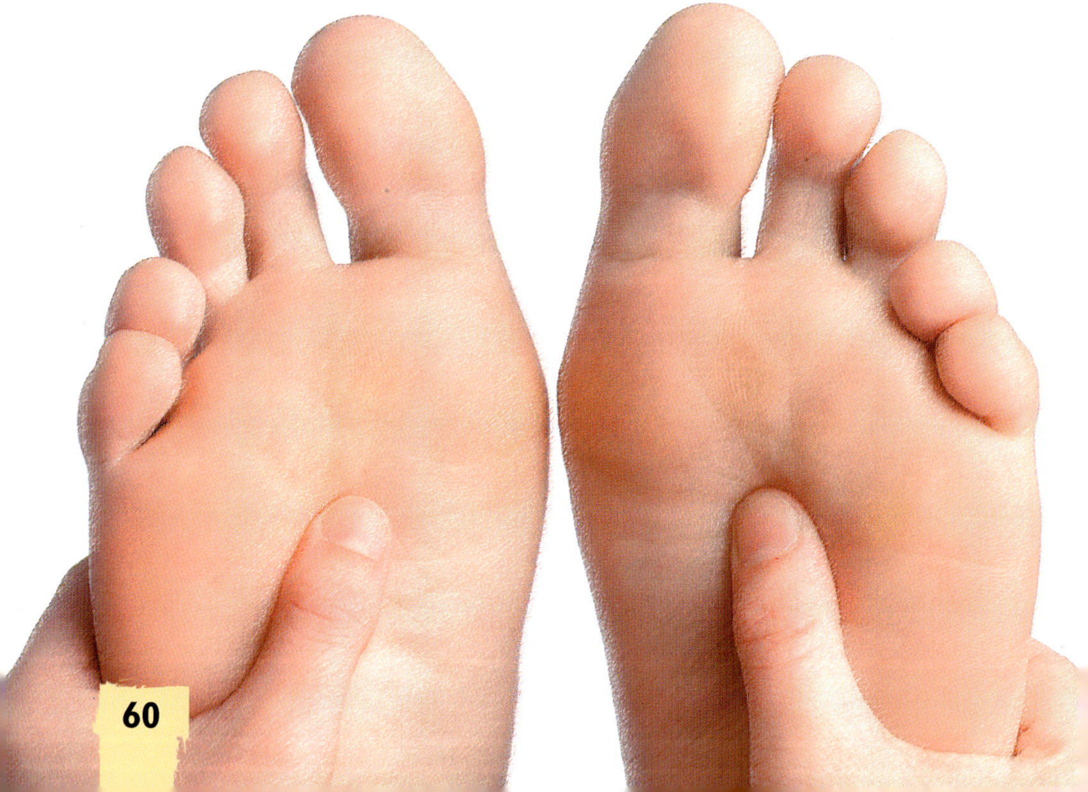

'spinal twist'

To alleviate any tension in the spine, especially when feeling a lot of neck and shoulder tension, it is good to use the 'spinal twist'.

This technique involves grasping the foot firmly in both hands along the spine reflex and twisting the foot as if wringing a cloth, taking great care not to move the skin rather than the foot itself.

Do not be alarmed if on some occasions the foot clicks as things shift back into place, but do take care not to inflict any injury to the recipient.

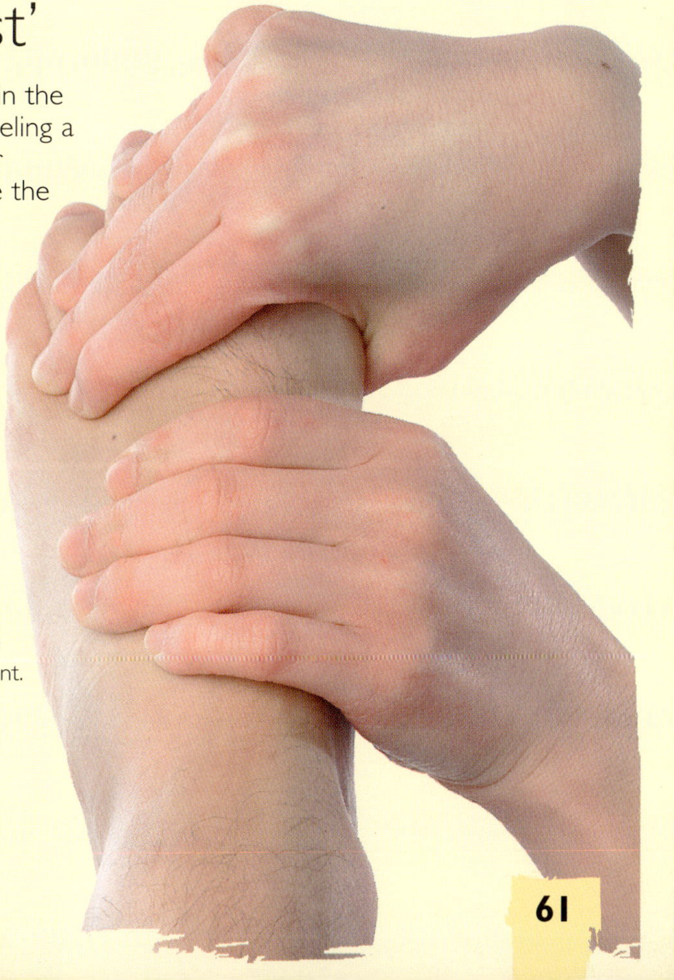

'relax shake'

A pleasant technique to open the treatment is the 'relax shake'.

This involves moving up and down either side of the foot simultaneously, using the palms of the hand. Each moves in the opposite direction and can be practised until you feel the tension in the feet has been released.

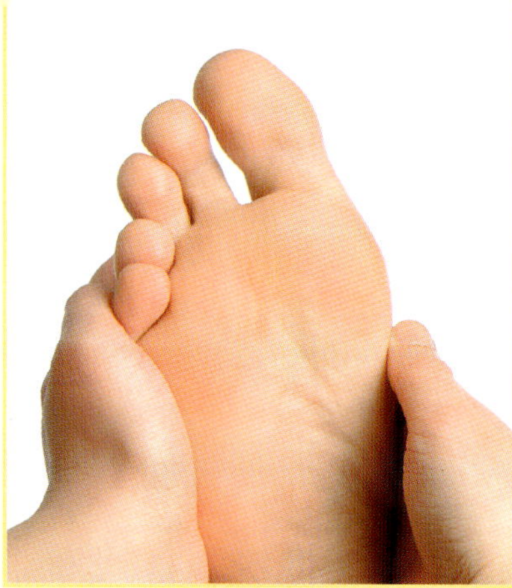

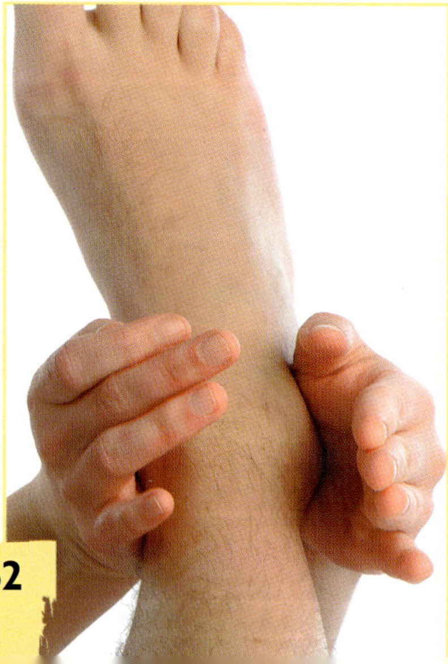

'ankle loosening'

'Ankle loosening' is another technique for alleviating tension within the foot but also works on a deeper level in the pelvic region too.

Cupping each side of the ankle on the bony ridge with the palms of your hands, gently move each hand forward alternately, creating a side-to-side movement of the foot.

* *Some caution should be exercised if the recipient is pregnant.*

'toe rotation'

Gently rotating each toe helps to ease the mind and clear the sinuses.

Gently pull each toe upwards and rotate anticlockwise, taking great care not to harm the toes themselves. Work each toe in turn, starting with the big toe.

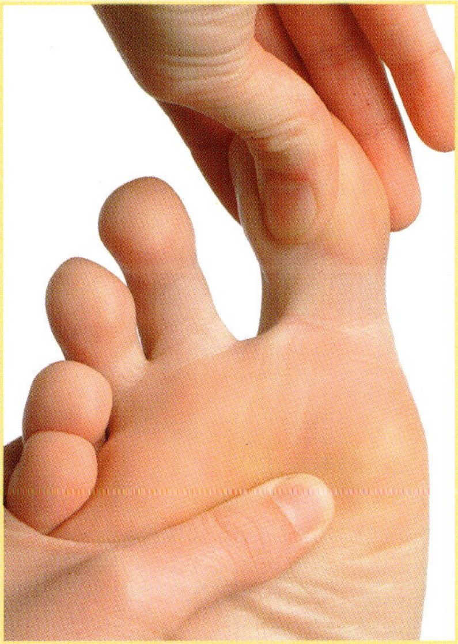

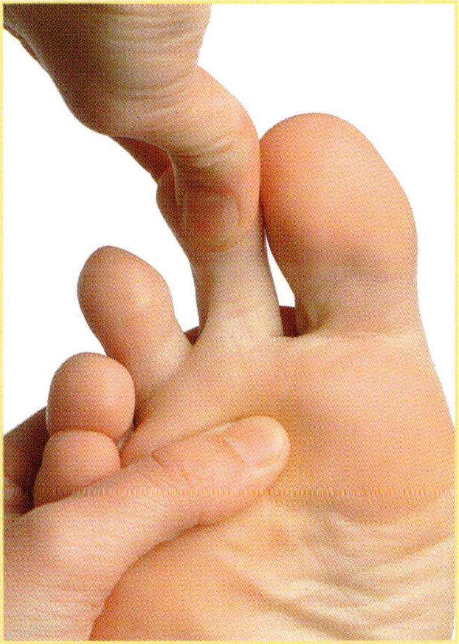

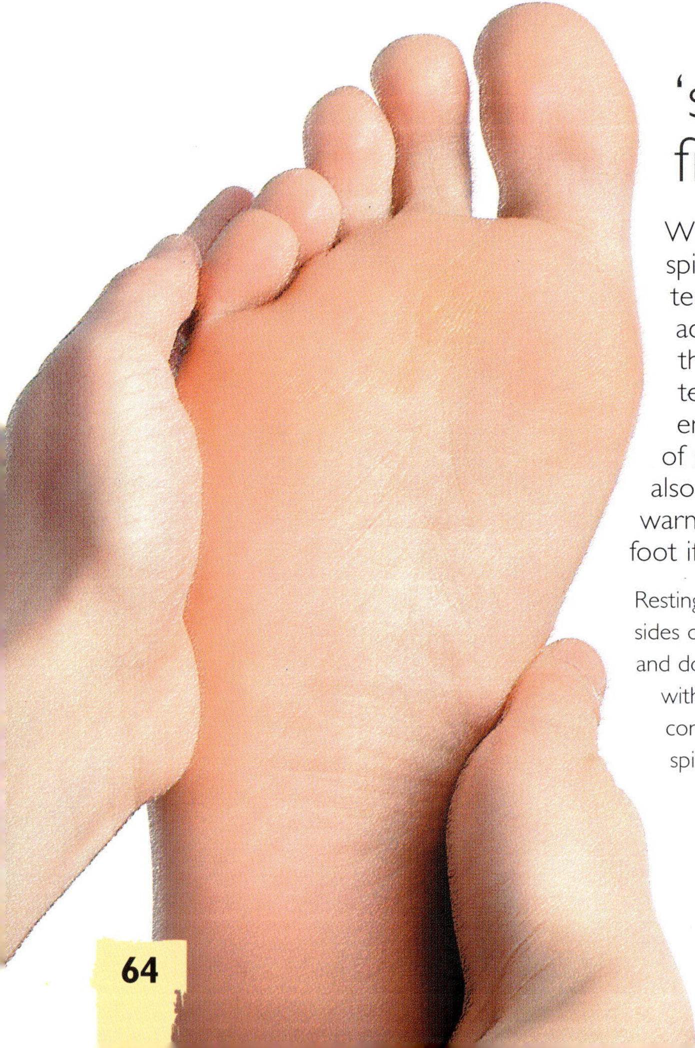

'spine friction'

When working on the spine and trying to move tension that may have accumulated in that area, the 'spine friction' technique not only encourages the release of muscular tension, but is also a good way of warming up the recipient's foot if feeling a bit cool.

Resting each palm against the sides of the feet, alternately run up and down the length of the foot with a brisk motion, if necessary, concentrating on the spine reflex.

‘ankle rotation’

Loosening the ankle and the pelvis can be achieved by using the ‘ankle rotation’ technique.

This is achieved by gripping the top of the foot with one hand on the lateral aspect, and cupping the heel with the other. Then move the top of the foot in a clockwise, circular motion, moving the bottom hand in an anti-clockwise direction. Only perform this movement if you feel that this is appropriate and can be achieved without causing any discomfort to the recipient.

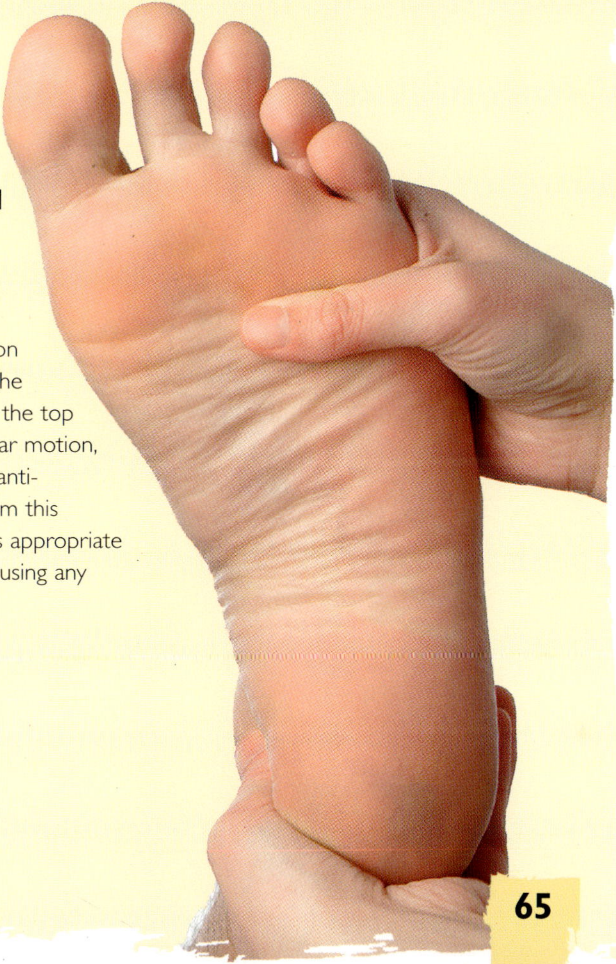

General **relaxation**

These techniques make a perfect rescue routine for relieving stress and tension, promoting relaxation and a restful sleep.

The techniques in combination make a good starting point for any of the following rescue routines, clearing the mind, and relaxing the body.

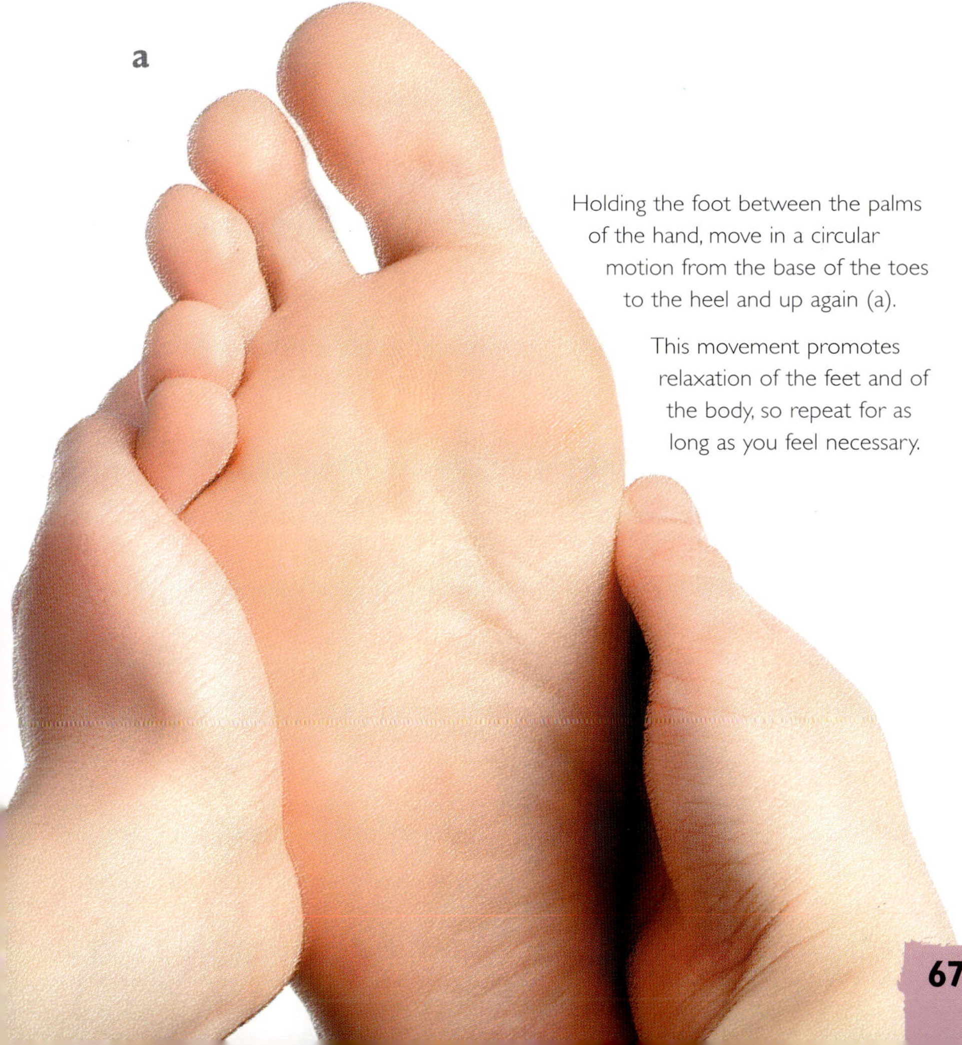

a

Holding the foot between the palms of the hand, move in a circular motion from the base of the toes to the heel and up again (a).

This movement promotes relaxation of the feet and of the body, so repeat for as long as you feel necessary.

b

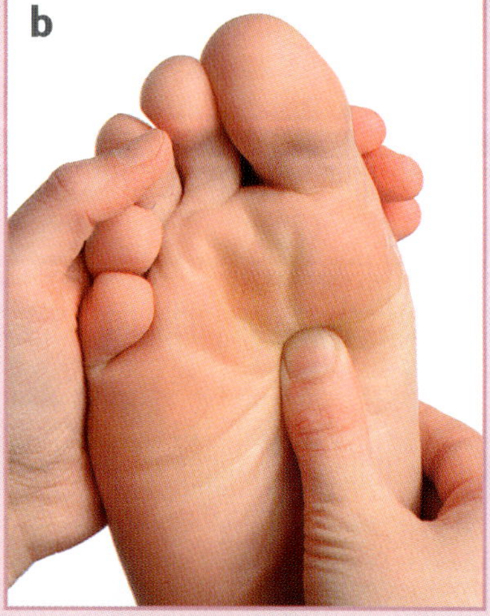

Gripping the foot with one hand, apply pressure with the thumb travelling along the diaphragm line (b), working from the inside (medial aspect) of the foot to the outer edge (lateral aspect), then returning back.

As you apply pressure with the thumb, (c) gently bring the upper portion of the foot towards you with the other hand, releasing as the thumb releases (d). This promotes deeper and easier breathing, easing both mind and body.

c

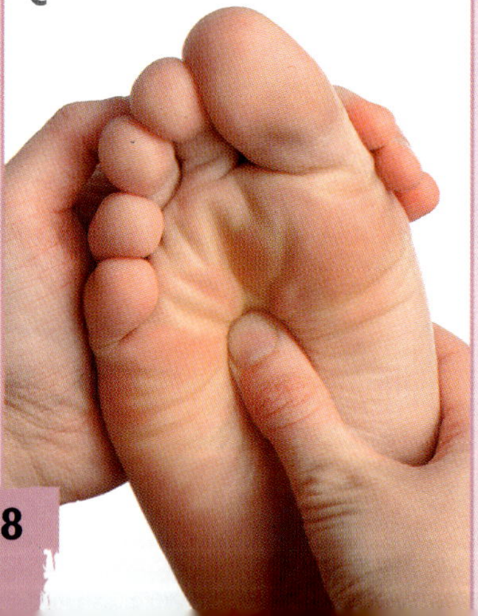

d

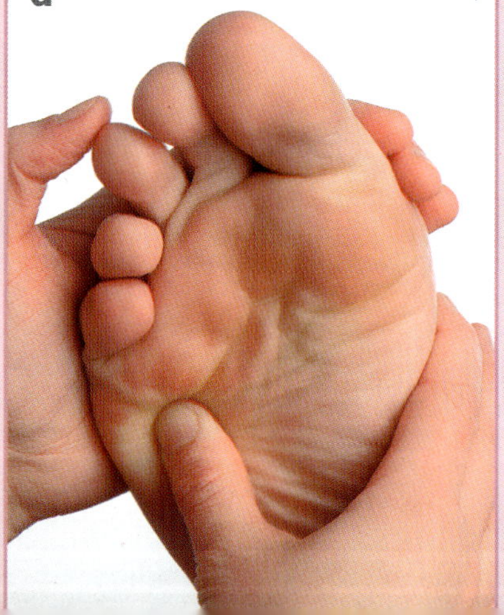

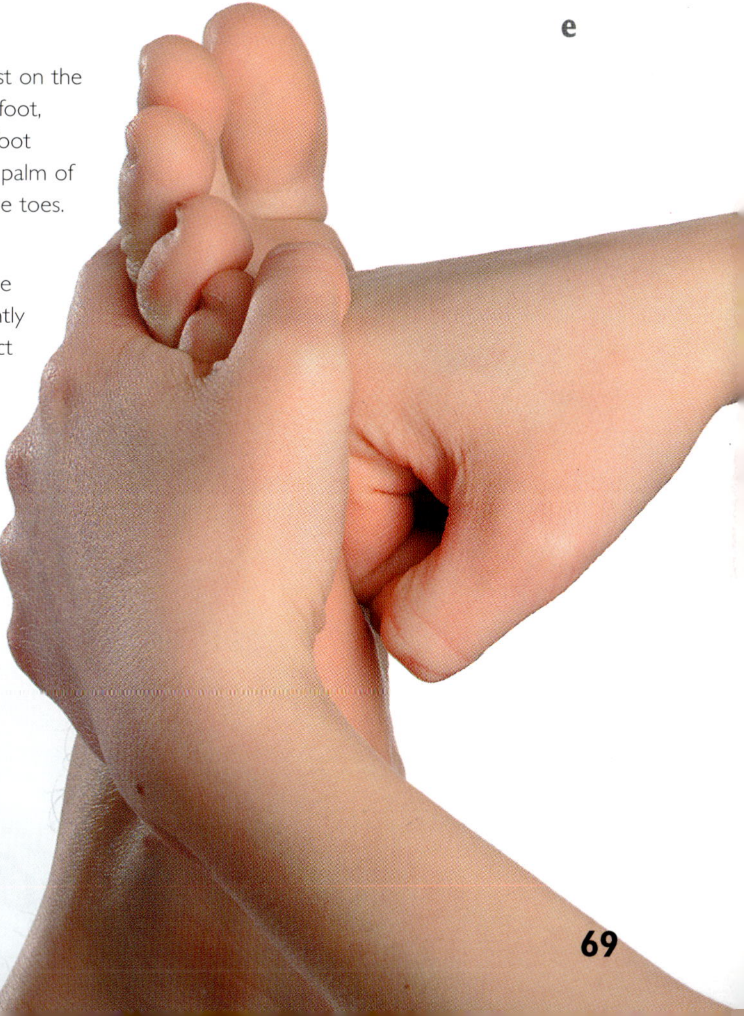

Holding the flat of the fist on the bottom (plantar) of the foot, support the top of the foot (dorsal aspect) with the palm of the hand just beneath the toes.

Push against the plantar aspect with the flat of the fist, release, and then gently squeeze the dorsal aspect in reply (e).

This is a very soothing movement and is a favourite with many so you can continue for as long as appropriate.

Holding both thumbs together in the middle of the plantar aspect of the foot beneath the line of the diaphragm (f), apply pressure with the thumbs while sweeping outwards from the centre of the foot (g), travelling down to the base of the heel.

f

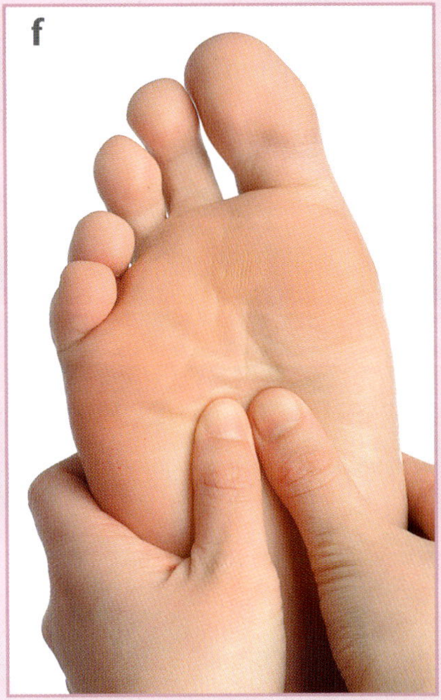

g

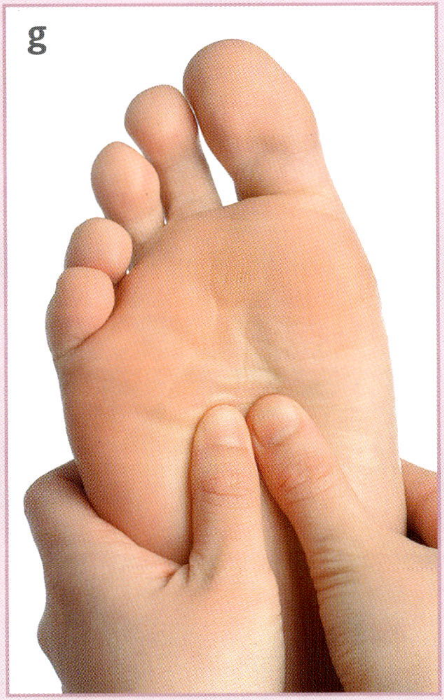

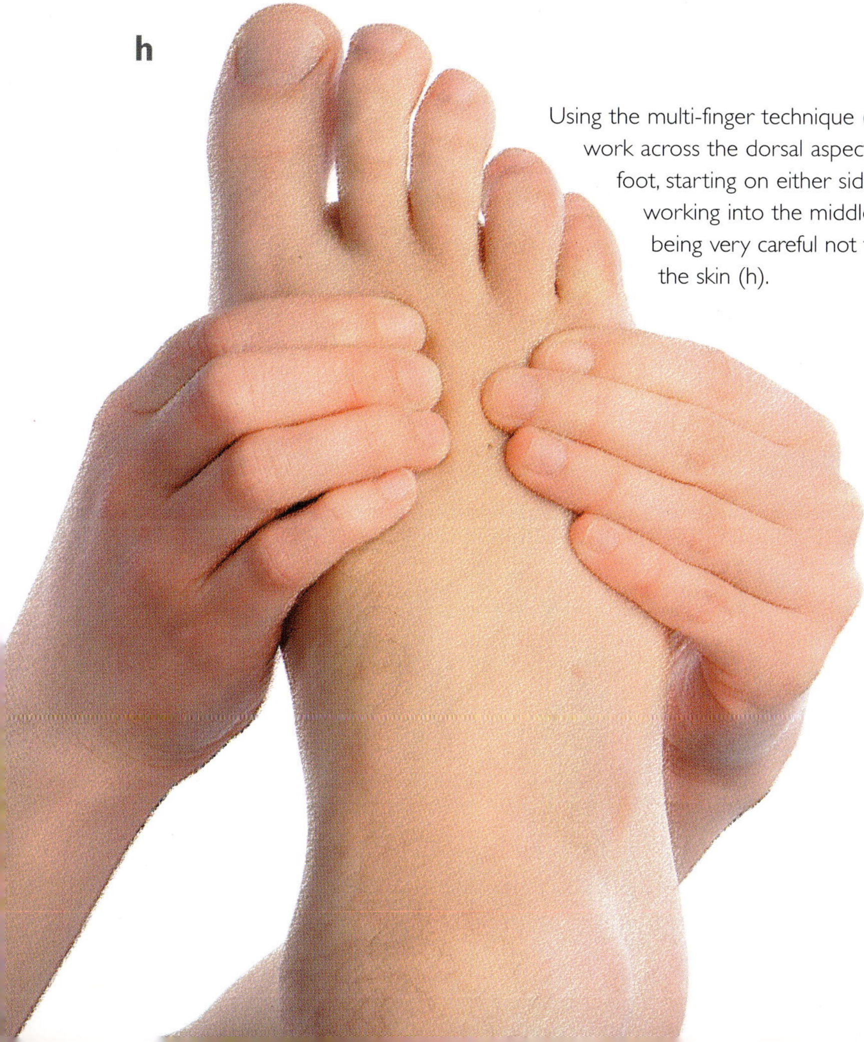

h

Using the multi-finger technique (p.57), work across the dorsal aspect of the foot, starting on either side and working into the middle – being very careful not to nip the skin (h).

i

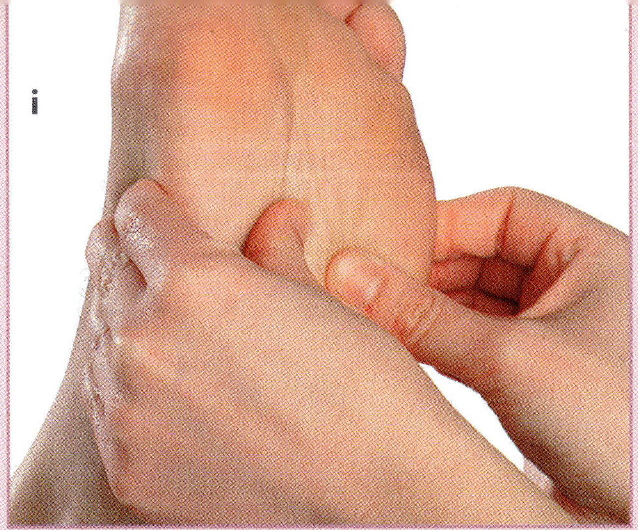

j

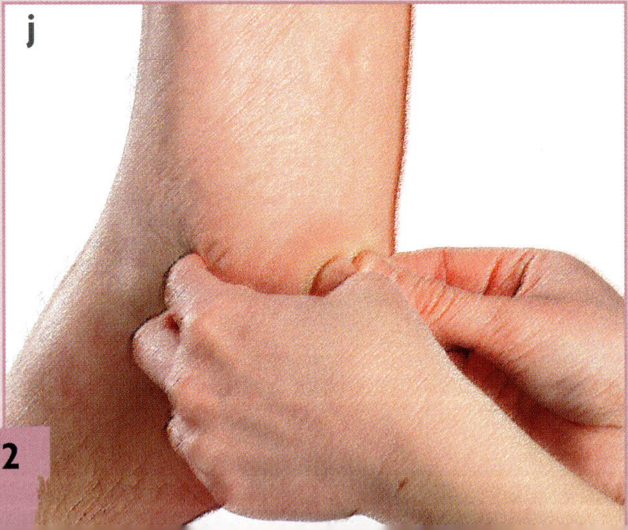

Concentrating on the edges of the feet, but following the spine reflex on the medial edge, make small circular movements with the tips of the fingers (i), moving from the base of toes to the base of the spine reflex (j).

Repeat three to five times, synchronising the movement of the two hands.

k

End the treatment by massaging the solar plexus area with the thumbs (k), gently holding the point for a time to balance the energies before releasing the feet.

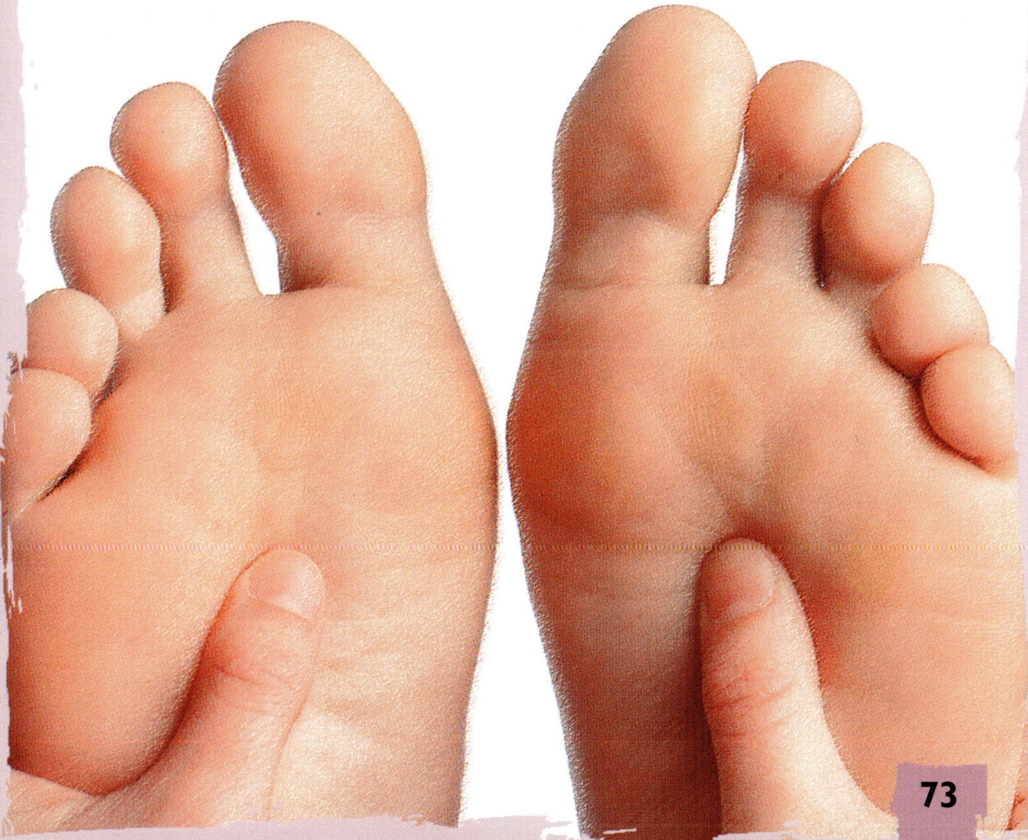

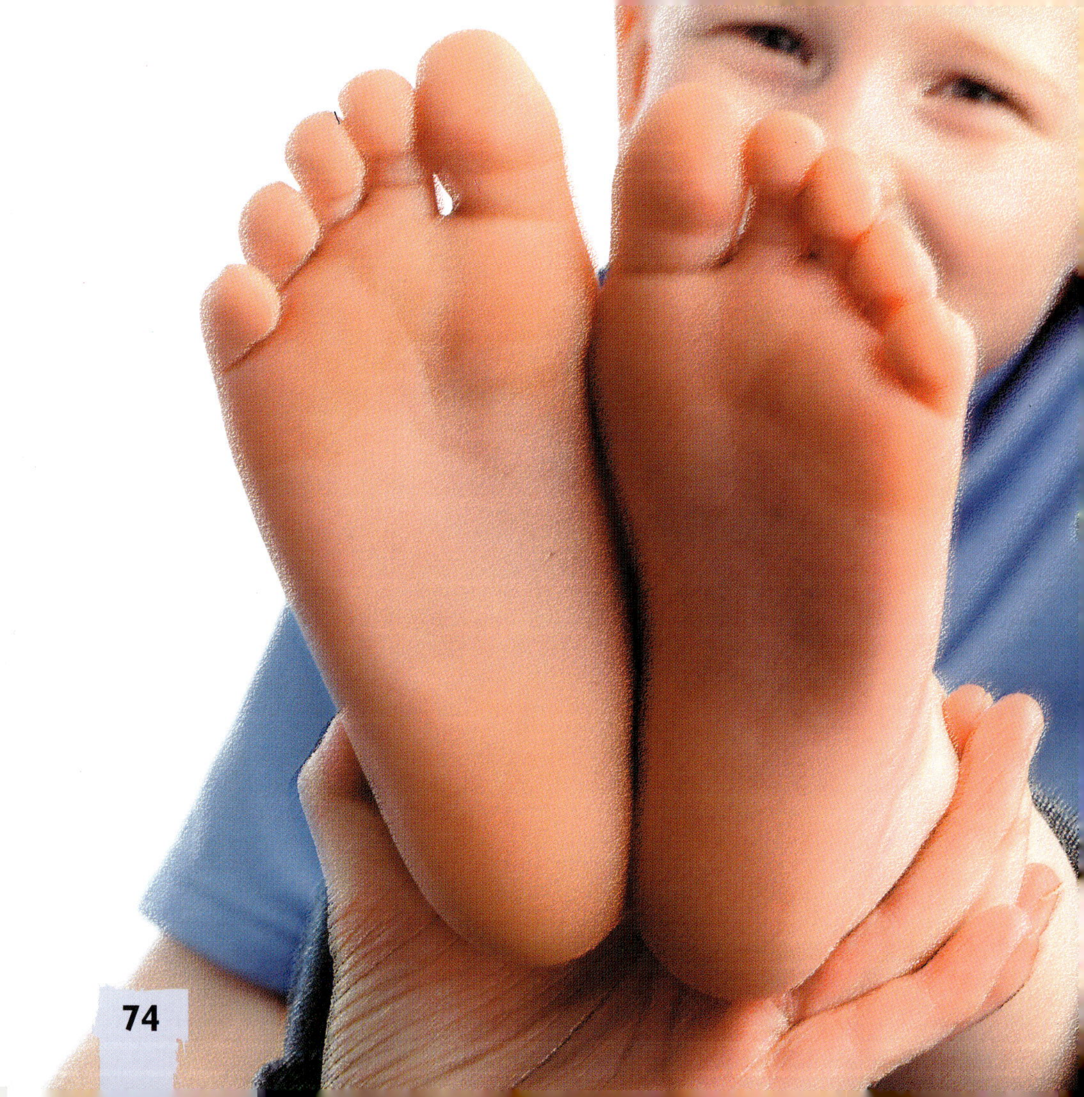

Baby and toddler soother

Reflexology treatment given to babies and children not only helps strengthen the bond between those involved, it also promotes relaxation, soothing both parent and child and encouraging healthy development of the child's sense of self and their identity.

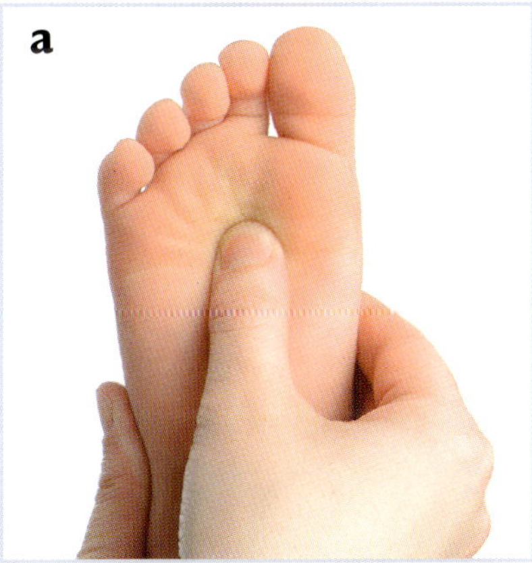

The treatment obviously needs to be quite short in length and much lighter pressure is needed when working the reflexes. This routine focuses on relaxing and easing tension and anxiety, working gently over the abdominal area to help sooth any tummy problems and aid digestion.

Using the thumbs slowly and gently, rotate over the solar plexus reflex on both feet, stroking across the diaphragm line every so often. These movements will help ease breathing (a).

Slowly and lightly move over the abdominal area and the heel using small circular movements of the thumb, beginning on the medial edge and working across to the lateral side (b).

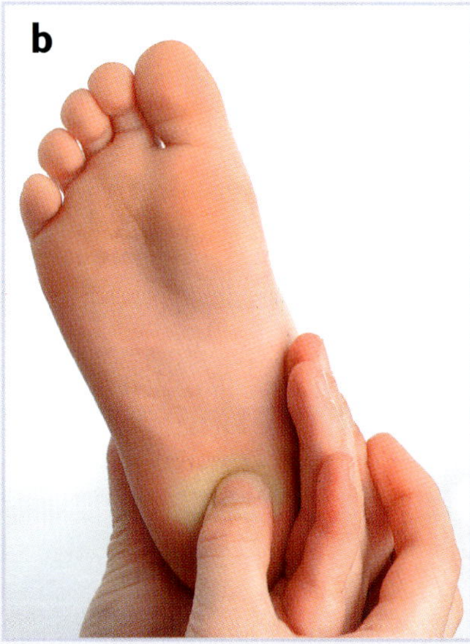

Focusing on the pads of the toes, use small and very gentle circular movements to help calm the mind (c).

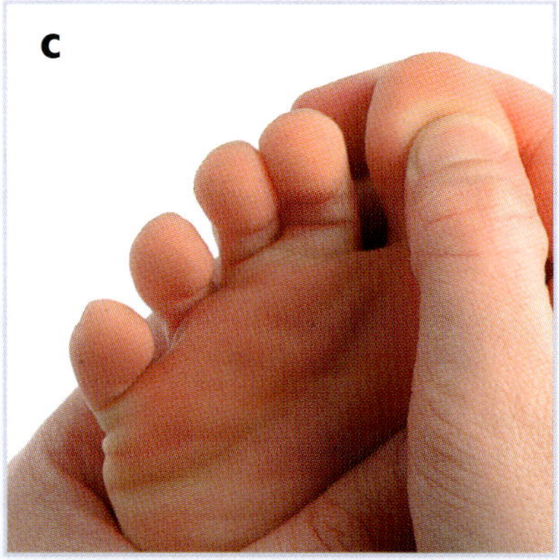

Continue with the small, circular movements along the spine reflex using a light touch, starting at the base of the big toenail and continue to the end of the reflex (d).

The size of the feet may allow you to treat both at the same time, which promotes a sense of harmony and is very soporific for the baby or child being treated. When ending the treatment, it is good to return to the solar plexus and hold the reflex for a short time to balance the body's energies.

d

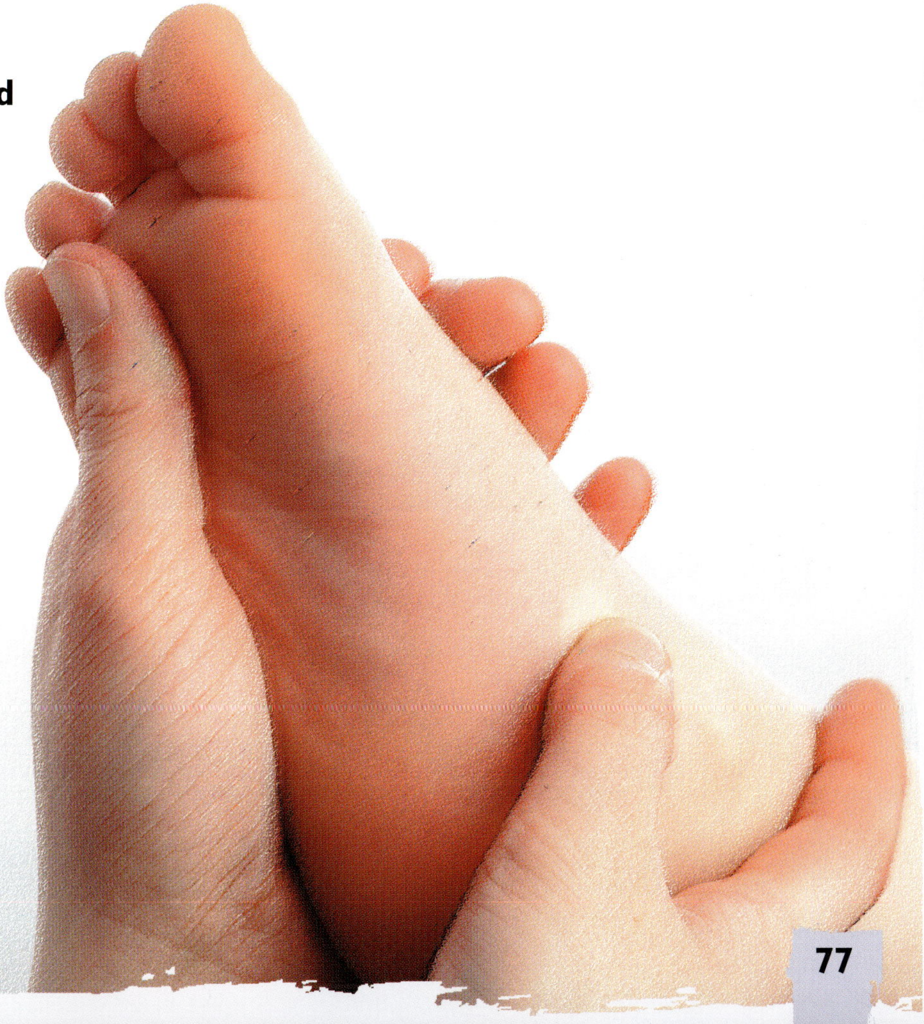

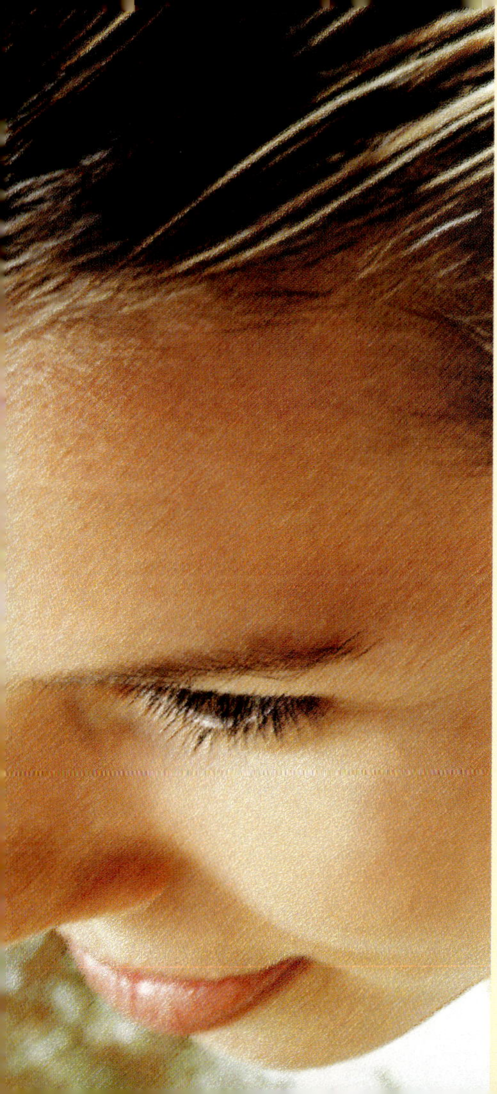

Headaches, NECK and shoulders

The hectic pace of life and work, combined with poor posture, often leads to headaches and tension in the head, neck and shoulders.

This routine will help to alleviate any tension that may have been allowed to accumulate in these areas and is best combined with the relaxation techniques listed earlier.

Using the caterpillar walking technique, work the plantar and dorsal shoulder reflexes.

The plantar shoulder reflex is worked vertically from the diaphragm up to the base of the toes in order to feel the pockets of congestion, which reflect the muscular tension (a).

a

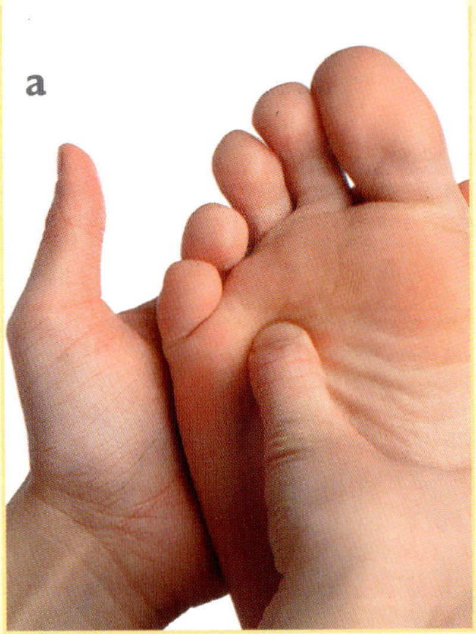

b

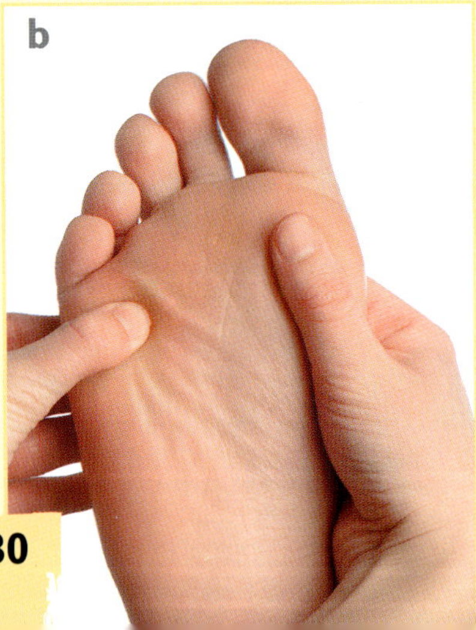

The shoulder reflexes on both sides can then be worked horizontally moving from the lateral edge inwards. Particular attention should be paid to the area directly beneath the toes on the plantar aspect, as congestion is apt to gather there if the tension is held high in the shoulders (b).

The dorsal aspect of the big toe reflects the face and working gently across this area, horizontally from the medial to lateral aspect, may help to alleviate tension in the head and sinuses (c).

c

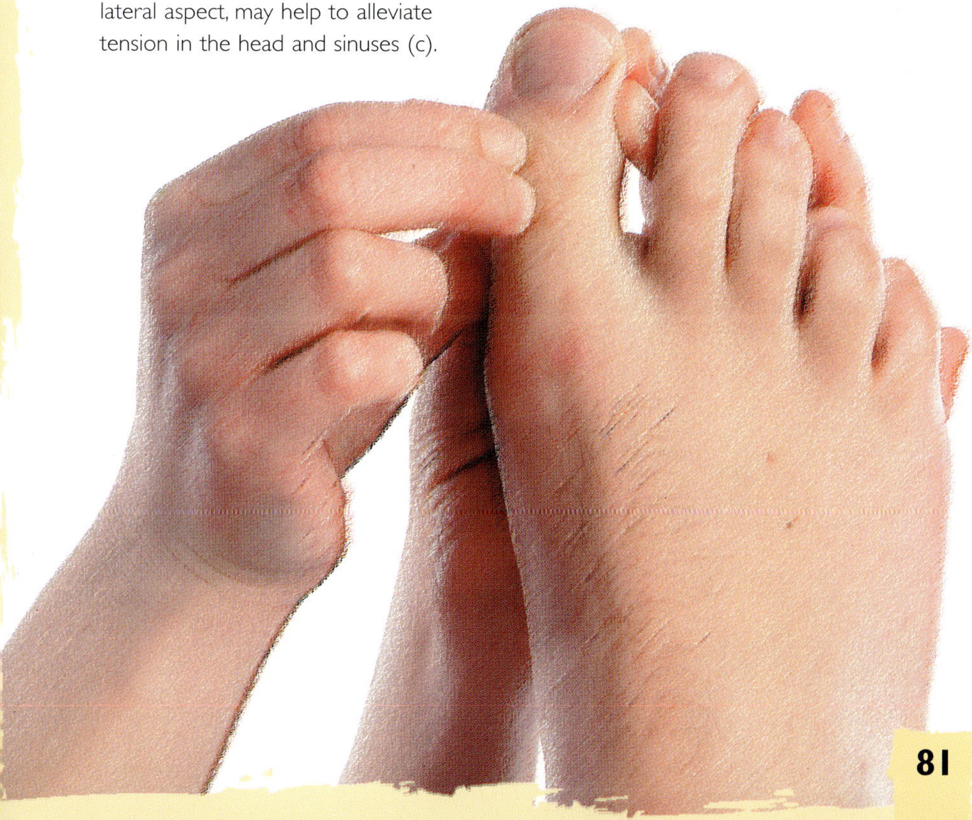

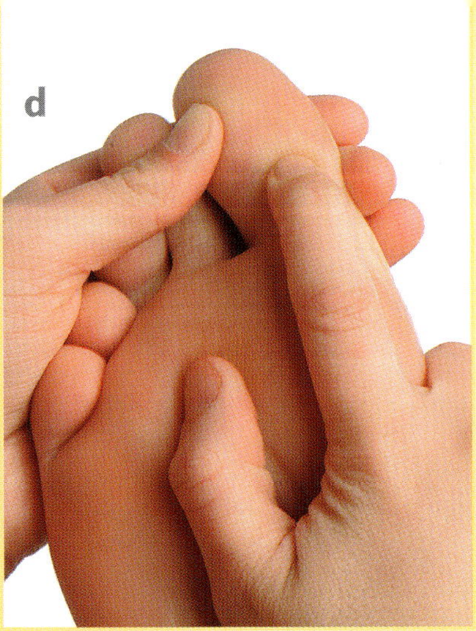

The big toe reflects the head and neck. The neck is found at the base of the toe and should be worked very carefully. If a large area of congestion is found, a small shock may be felt by the recipient (d).

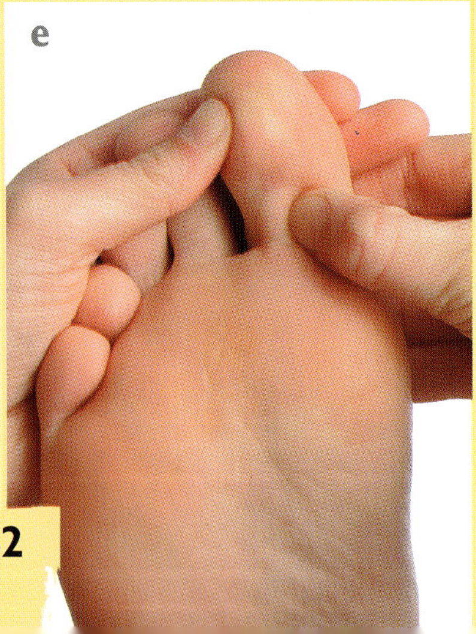

Using the caterpillar walking technique on the plantar aspect, it is best to travel vertically from the base to the tip of the toe and carefully work your way across from the medial to the lateral aspect (e).

If a large obstruction is found, it is sometimes better to work horizontally across the neck reflex.

f

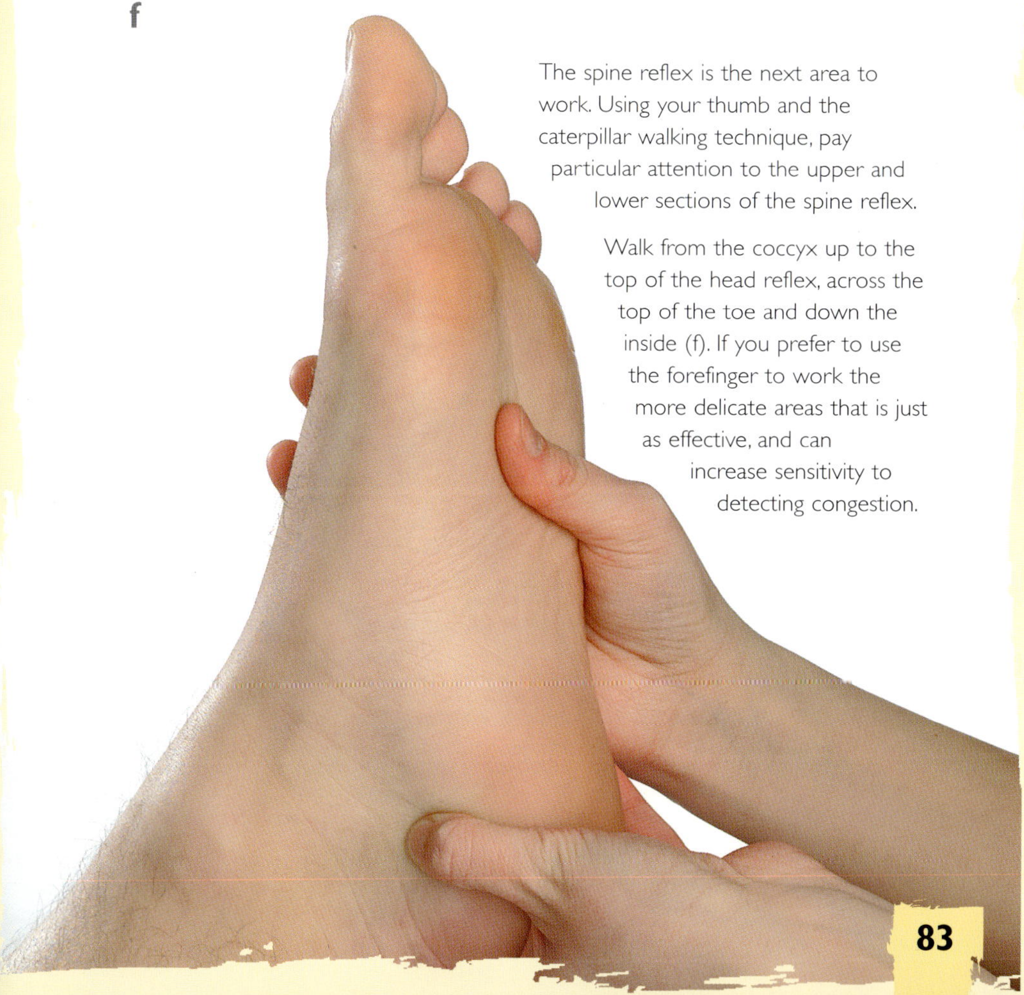

The spine reflex is the next area to work. Using your thumb and the caterpillar walking technique, pay particular attention to the upper and lower sections of the spine reflex.

Walk from the coccyx up to the top of the head reflex, across the top of the toe and down the inside (f). If you prefer to use the forefinger to work the more delicate areas that is just as effective, and can increase sensitivity to detecting congestion.

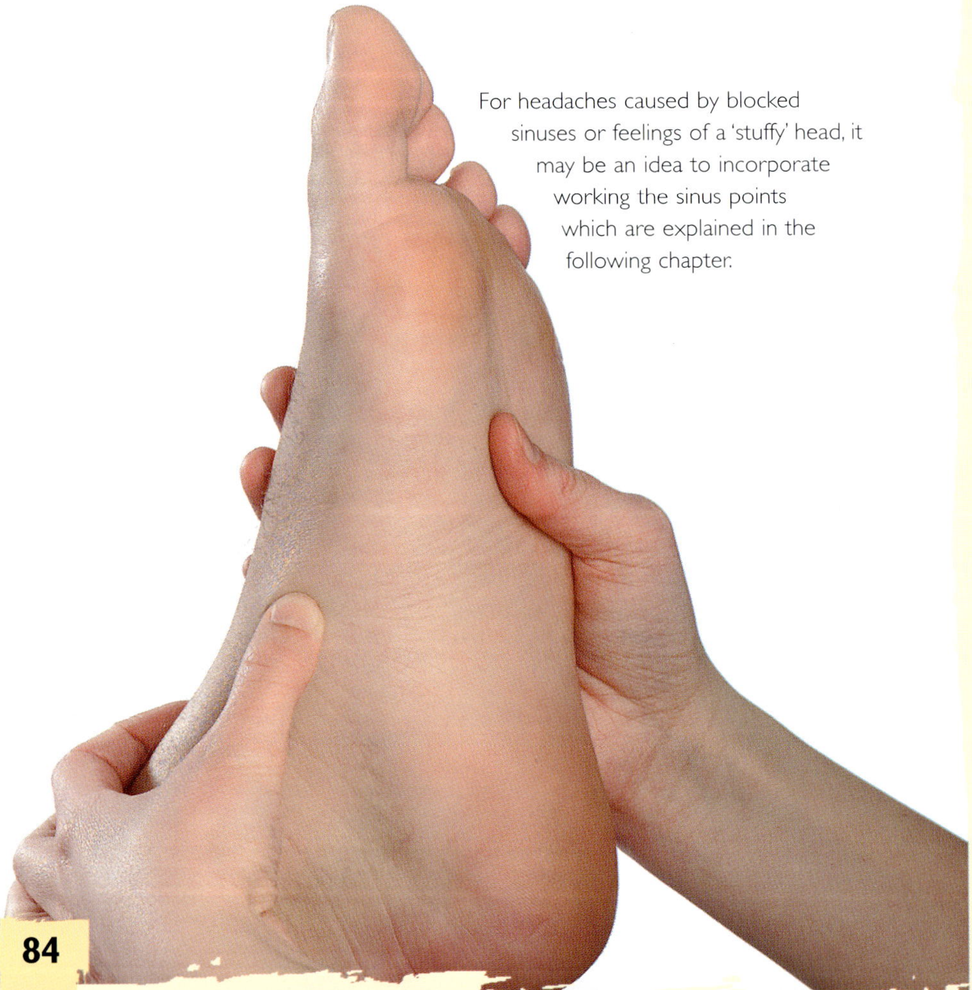

For headaches caused by blocked sinuses or feelings of a 'stuffy' head, it may be an idea to incorporate working the sinus points which are explained in the following chapter.

Supporting the foot, use your thumb or forefinger to trace back down along the spine. The change of direction allows for a greater stimulus of the spinal nerves and encourages further energy balancing.

Coughs, colds and FLU

Reflexology treatment can be effective in helping soothe and clear up any cold, cough or flu symptoms, whilst stimulating the body's response to illness and building up the immune system.

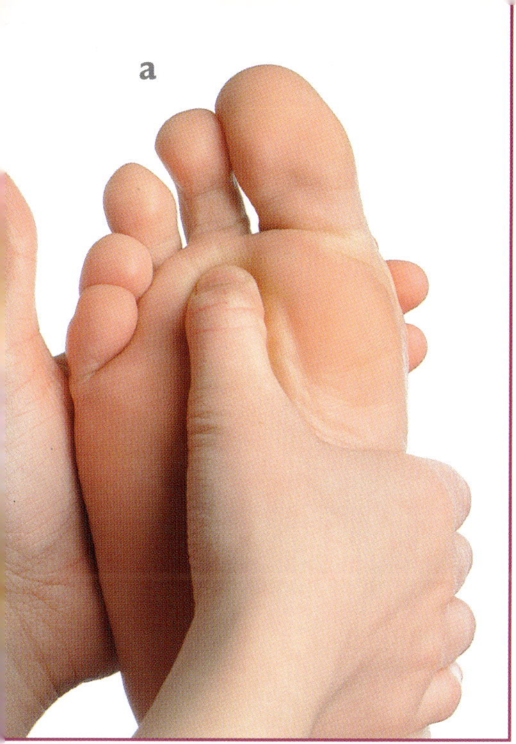

Pay particular attention to the trachea and the thymus reflexes as they may show some congestion, which will need encouragement to disperse (b).

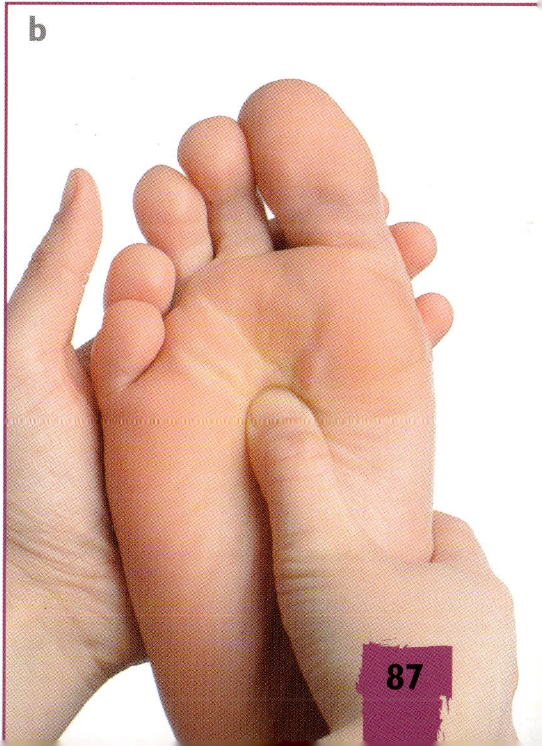

Using the thumb-walking method, work in vertical lines, moving up from the diaphragm line to the base of the toes, beginning at the medial edge moving across to the lateral edge and returning inwards (a).

The head and sinuses are found on the toes. Finger-walk vertically from base to tip, making sure the whole of the underside of each toe is covered. Work from the medial to the lateral edge and on the return, work from the lateral to the medial edge.

The sinuses can be quite congested and tender, so it is best to pay particular attention to reactions from the recipient. To stimulate the sinuses further, you may want to apply pressure to the point on the toe pads of the four little toes where the swelling is most prominent, usually around the mid-point where the curves grow more distinct.

Work across the dorsal chest and abdominal reflexes using the multi-fingered technique, taking care not to nip the skin.

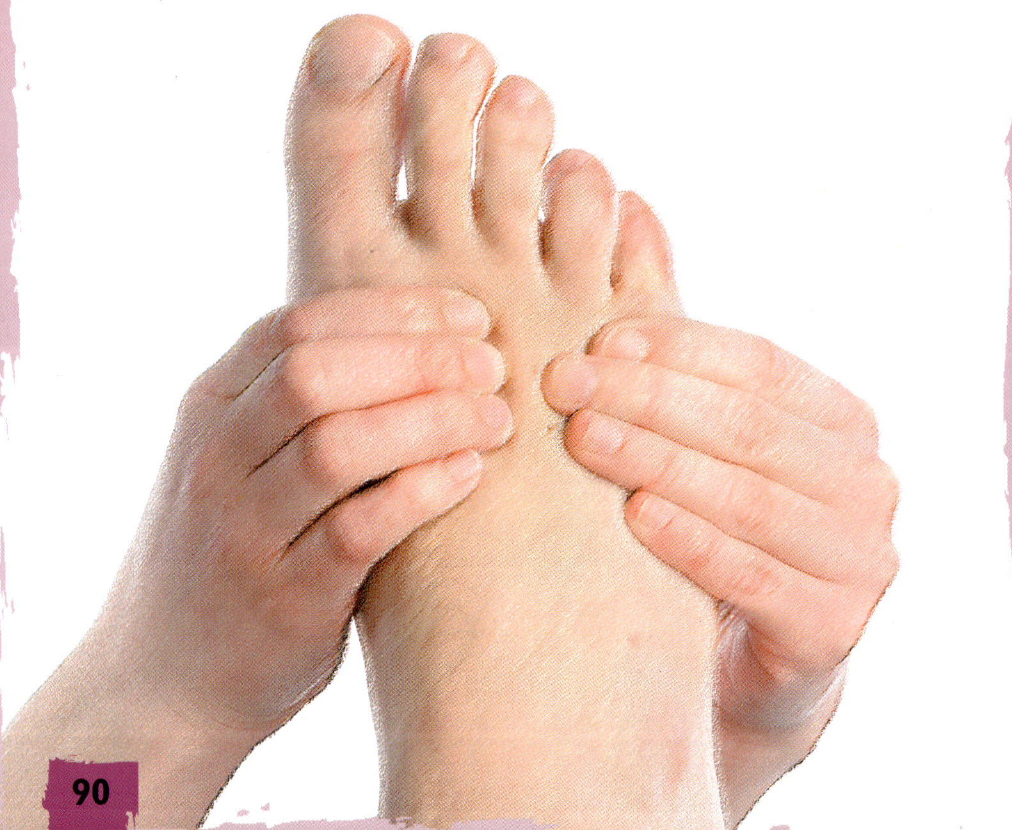

Gently massage the abdominal and pelvic area on the plantar aspect, using a circular motion with the thumb, from the medial to the lateral edge.

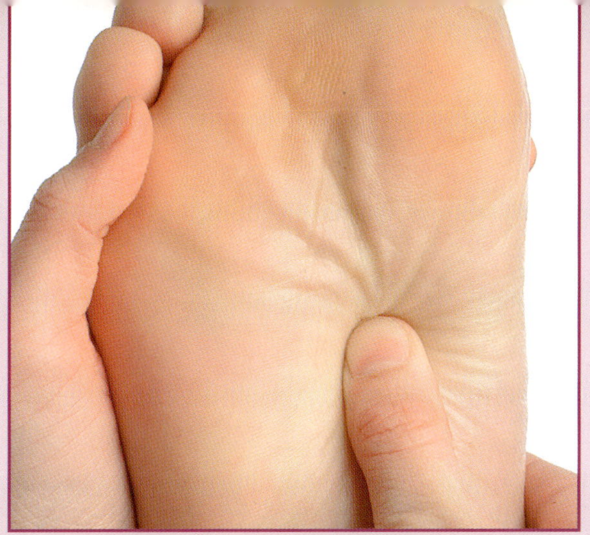

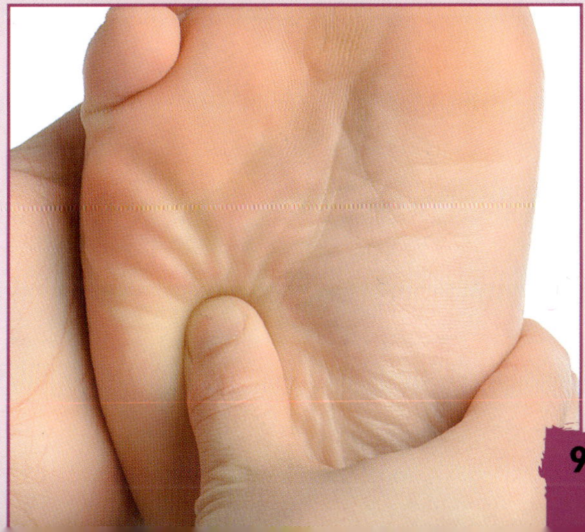

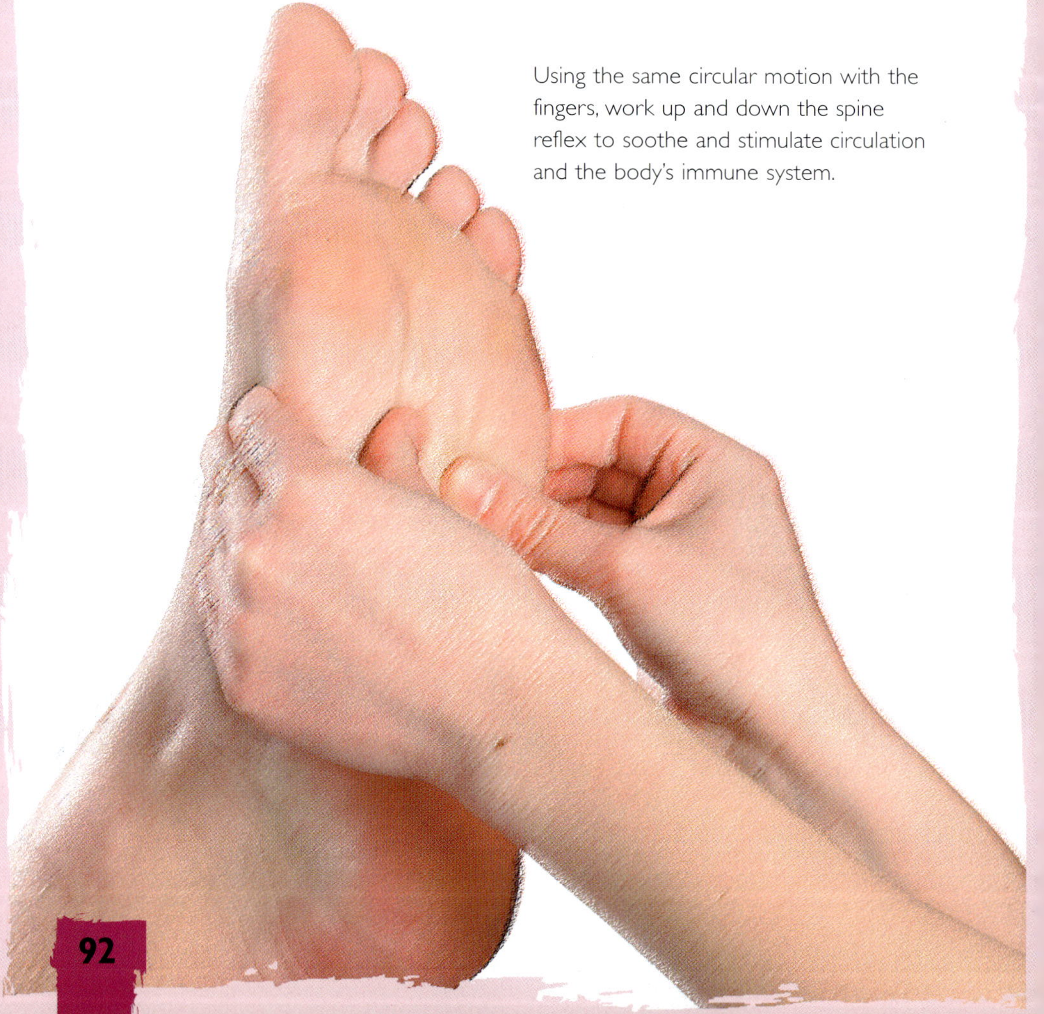

Using the same circular motion with the fingers, work up and down the spine reflex to soothe and stimulate circulation and the body's immune system.

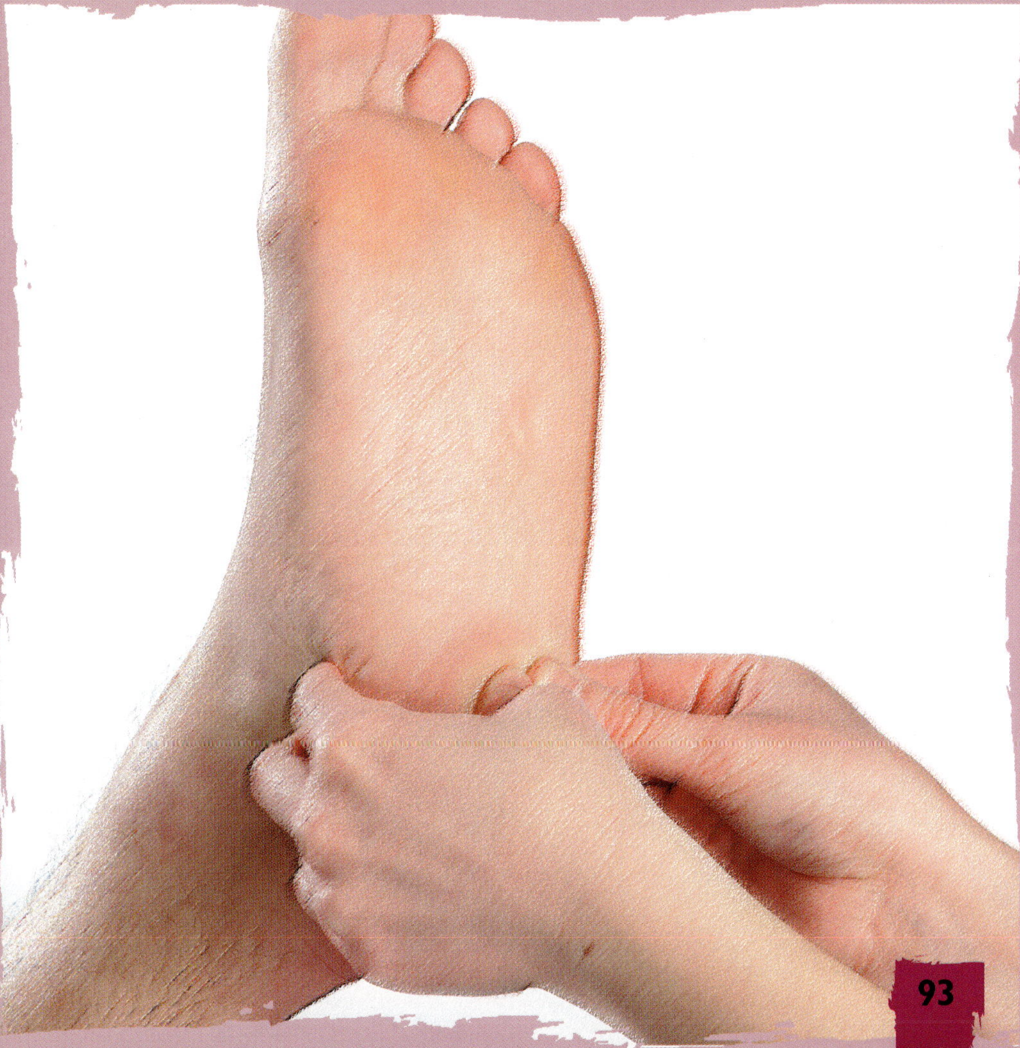

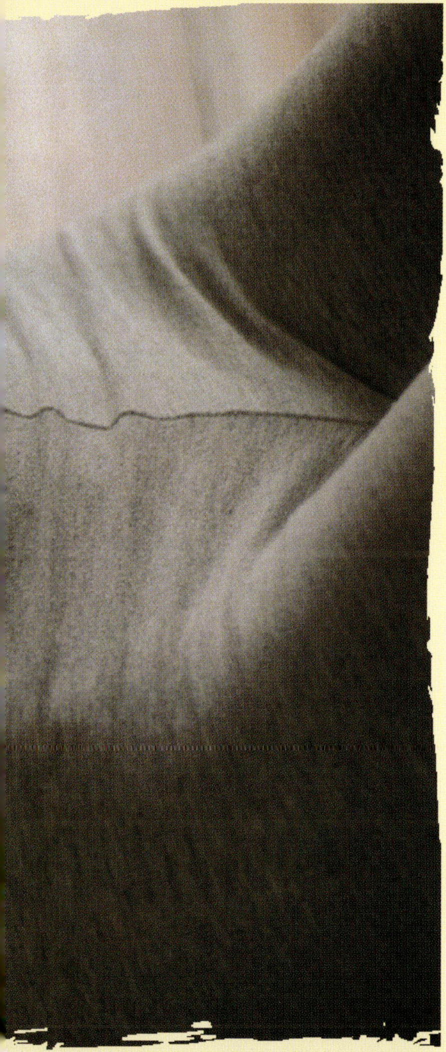

Stomach SOOTHER

Relaxation is important for healthy functioning of the body in general, but is especially important when eating and digesting food. Stress and tension greatly affect the stomach leading to the development of ulcers and contributing to irritable bowel syndrome.

Concentrating on the liver, stomach and pancreas reflexes (a), work diagonally across from the medial to the lateral edge of the foot using the thumb-walking technique (b), returning back to the centre and not travelling beneath the centre line of the foot (c).

This can be repeated on the left foot, which would then include the stomach, spleen and pancreas reflexes.

a

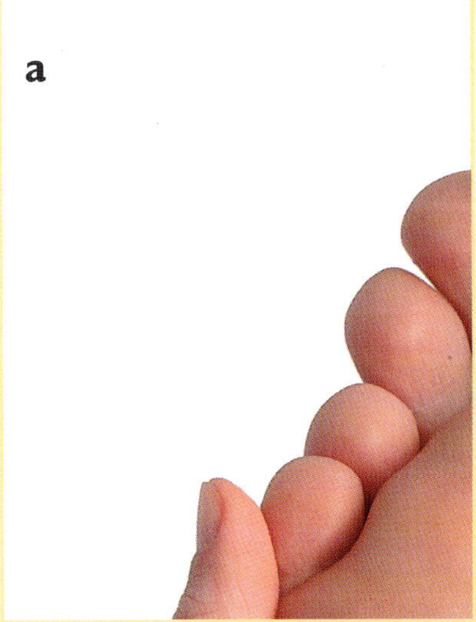

b

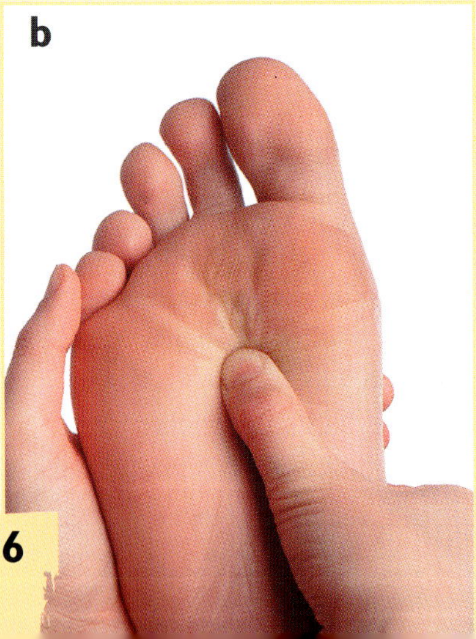

c

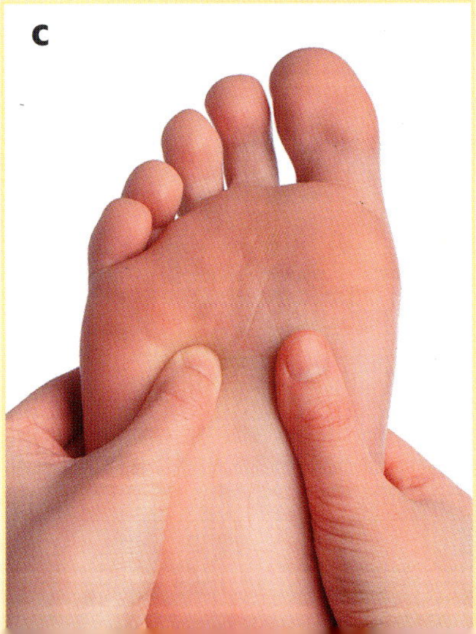

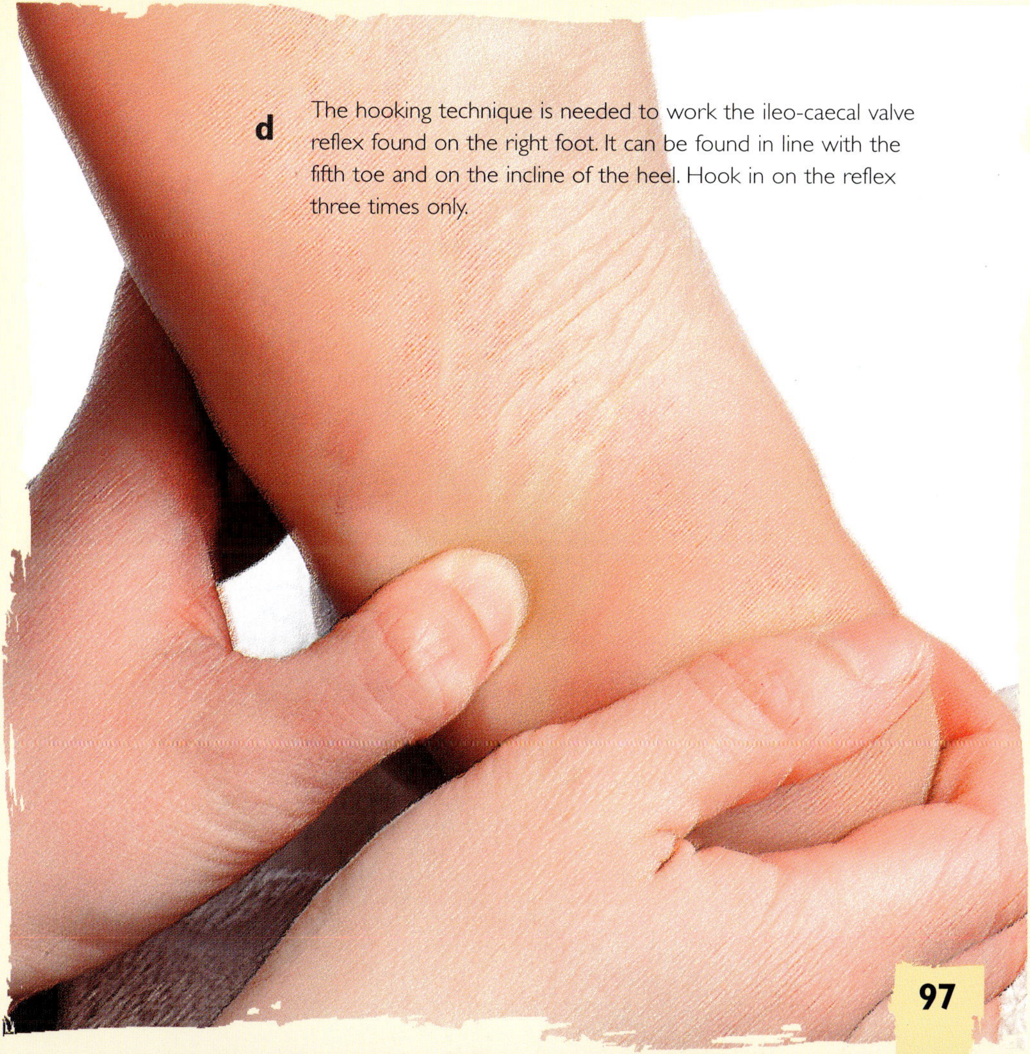

d The hooking technique is needed to work the ileo-caecal valve reflex found on the right foot. It can be found in line with the fifth toe and on the incline of the heel. Hook in on the reflex three times only.

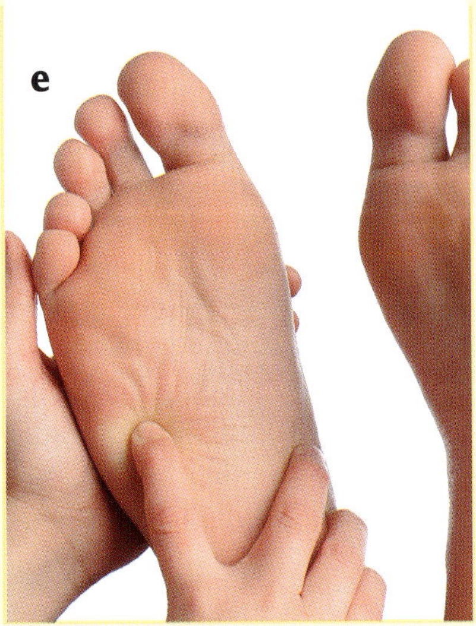

Follow the line of the large intestine reflexes on both feet using the finger walking technique to improve the release of tension and normal function of the intestine (e).

Begin on the ileo-cecal valve, travel up the first section of the large intestine on the right foot and follow the intestine along onto the left foot, stopping by the ileo-caecal reflex (f, g, h, i, j). This can be repeated a few times to improve function and soothe the abdomen.

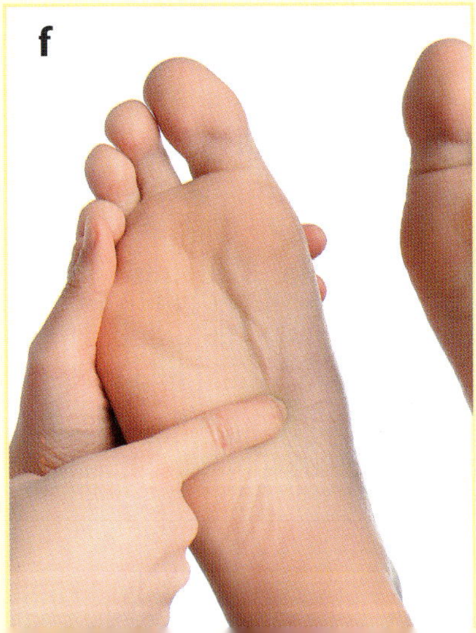

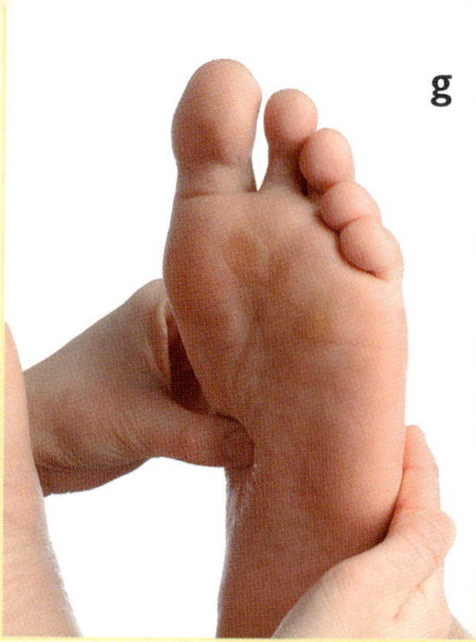
g

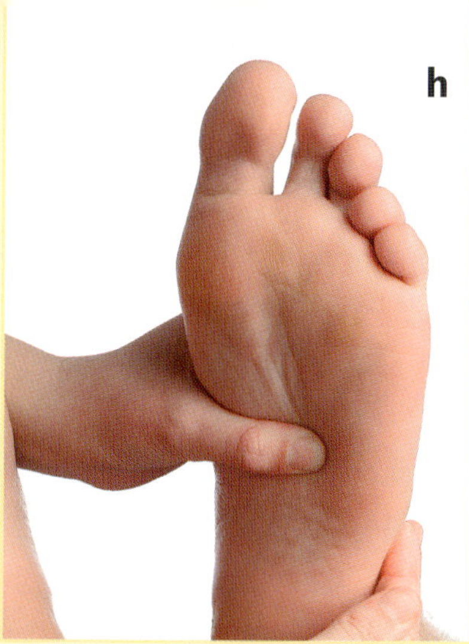
h

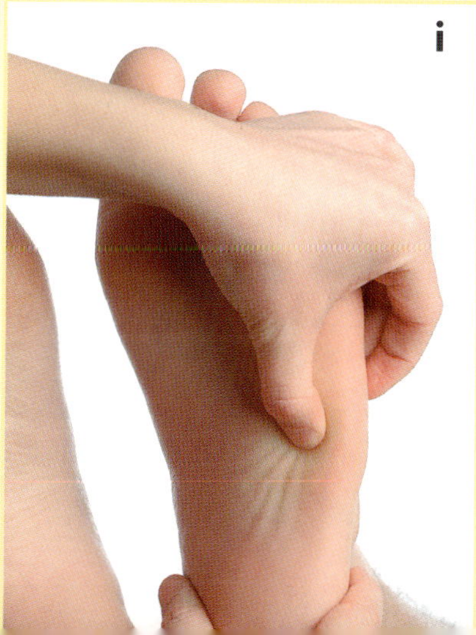
i

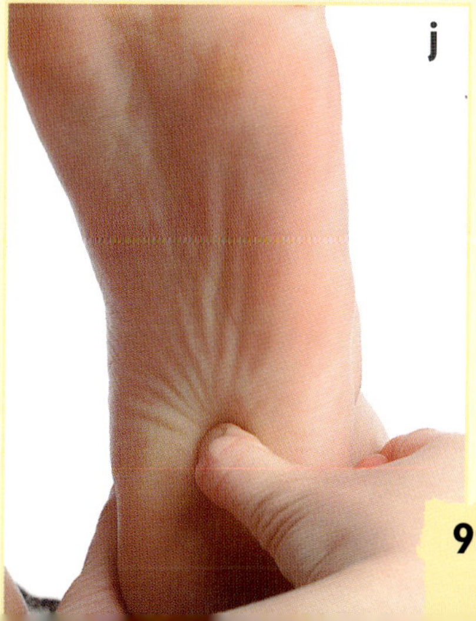
j

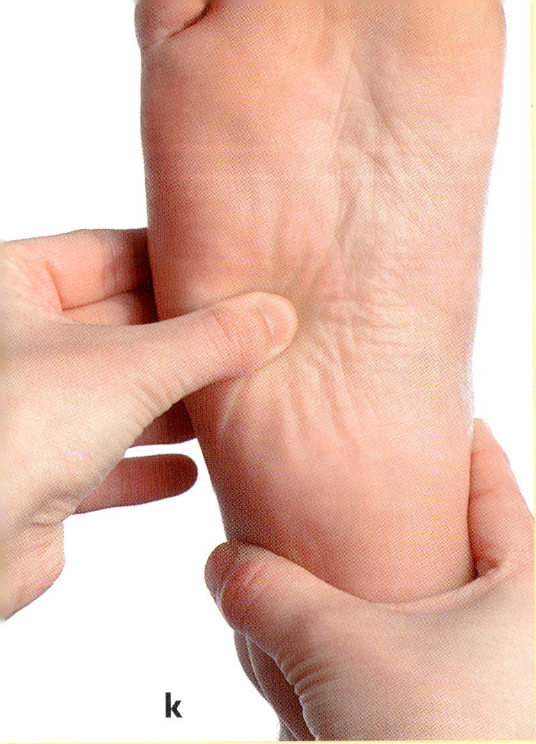

Work horizontally across the lower half of the feet from the mid-line down to the bottom of the heel. Use the thumb walking technique, from the medial to the lateral edge, to stimulate and soothe the general abdominal area (k).

Use the multi-fingered technique across the whole of the dorsal aspect of the foot to encourage the release of tension in the abdominal area. (l)

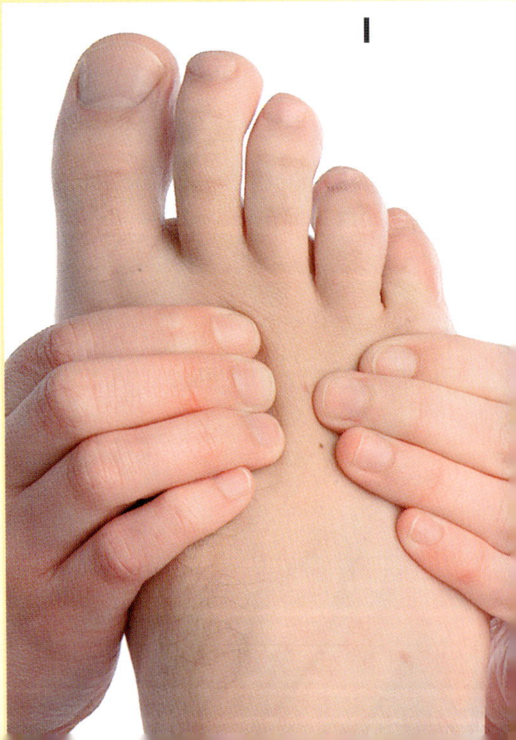

n

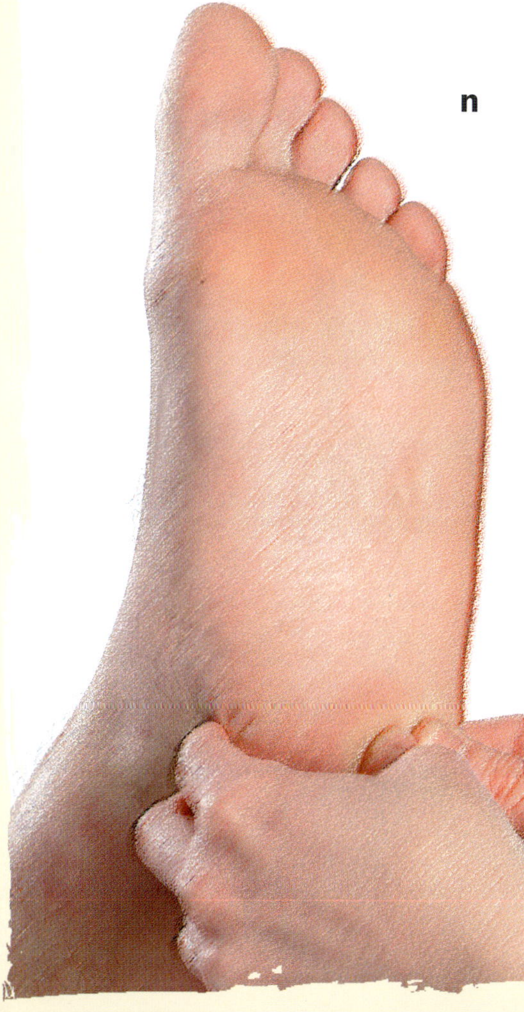

You may want to work along the spine reflex using a circular motion from the base of the big toe to the coccyx point on the heel. This will encourage movement within the energy meridians, efficient nerve communication, and general relaxation (m, n).

m

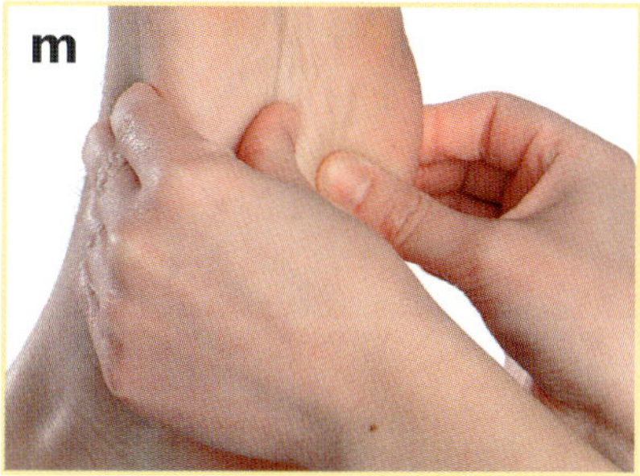

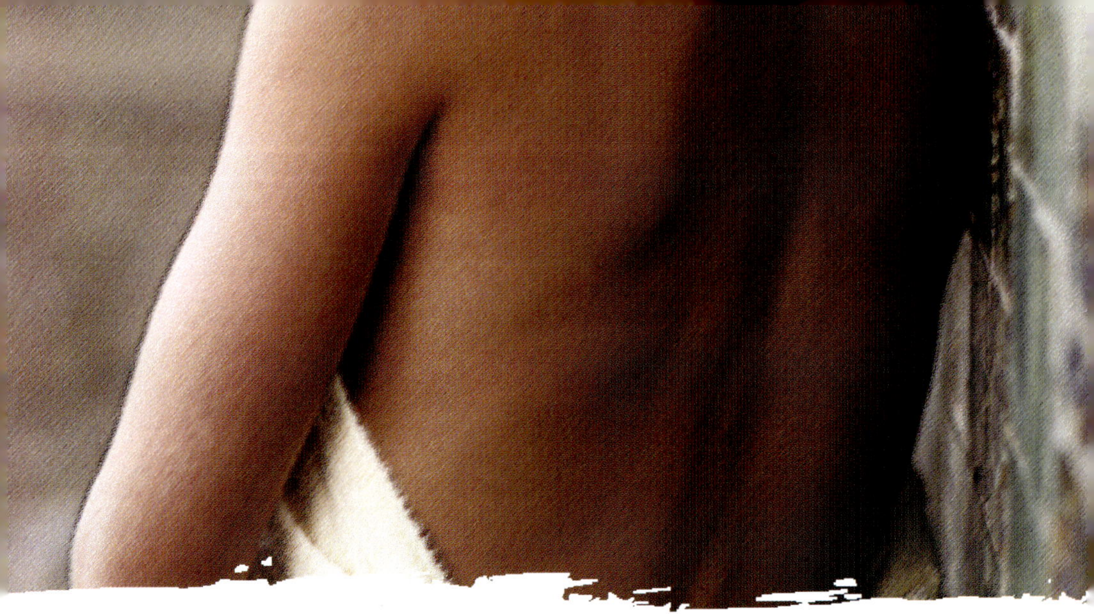

Spine and pelvis

Many people experience back problems whether as a result of poor posture, disc problems, degenerative conditions such as arthritis or osteoporosis, or simply muscular tension or trapped nerves. This routine has been devised with such problems in mind and it is hoped that the techniques may offer some relief. Serious conditions, however, should only be treated after seeking medical advice and then only by a qualified reflexologist.

a

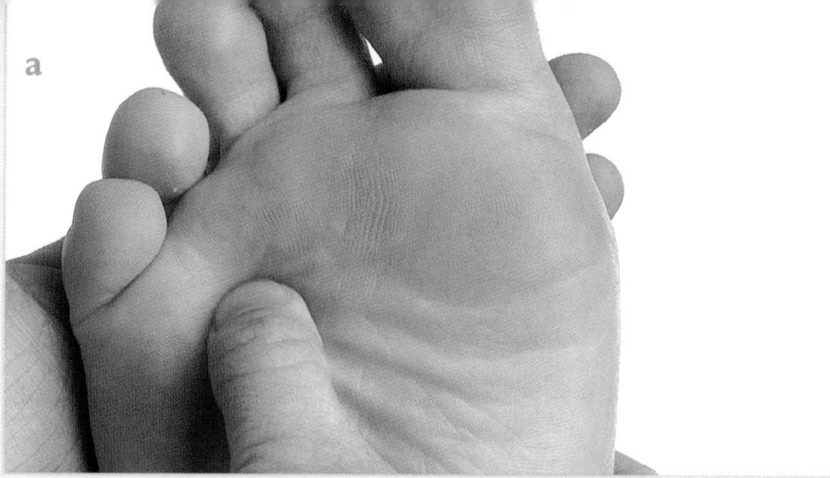

Start by working the shoulder reflex on the plantar aspect of the foot (a), with the thumb-walking technique. Travelling vertically from the diaphragm line to the base of the toes, work towards the lateral aspect of the foot (b).

b

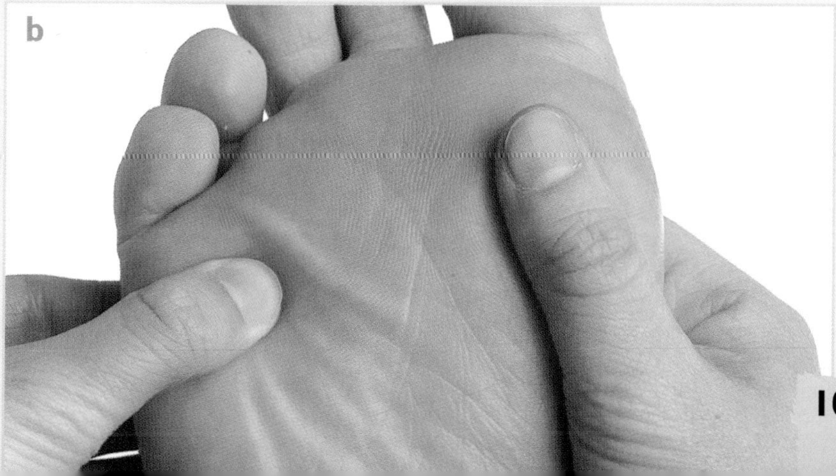

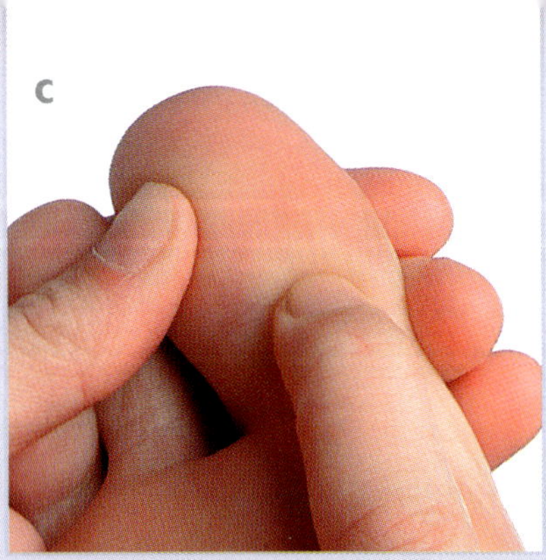

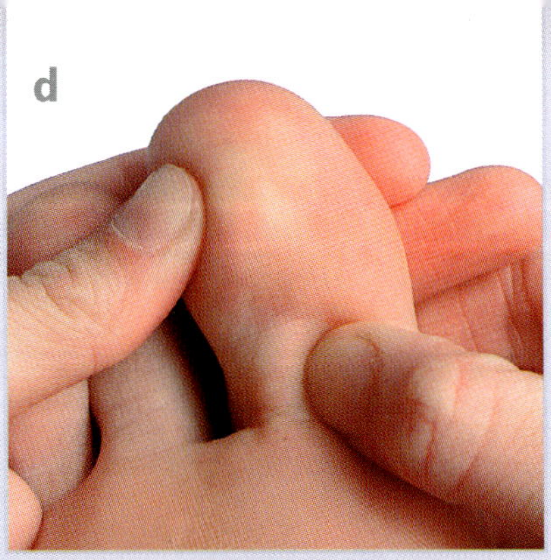

The neck reflex at the base of the big toe on the plantar aspect can be worked either by finger- or thumb-walking and it may be best to travel horizontally from the medial to the lateral edge (c, d).

The hip and pelvis reflexes on the medial and lateral aspects of the foot are best worked using the finger-walking technique and moving from the heel up in a semicircular movement underneath and behind the ankle bone (e).

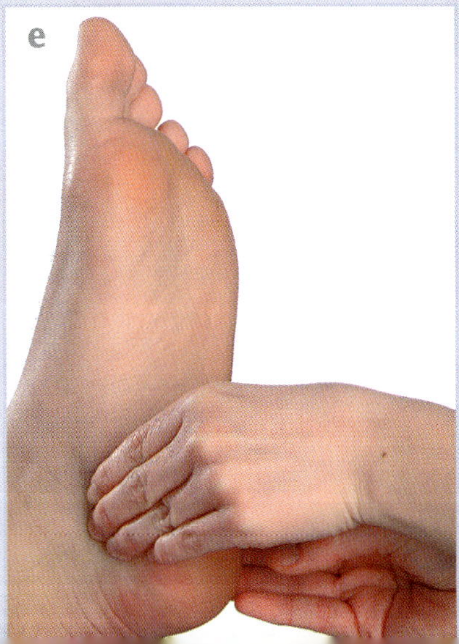

The spine reflex can be worked using the thumb- or finger-walking technique; whichever is more sensitive for you. Running from the coccyx up to the top of the head reflex and big toe, return down to the base of the spine reflex after three runs (f, g, h).

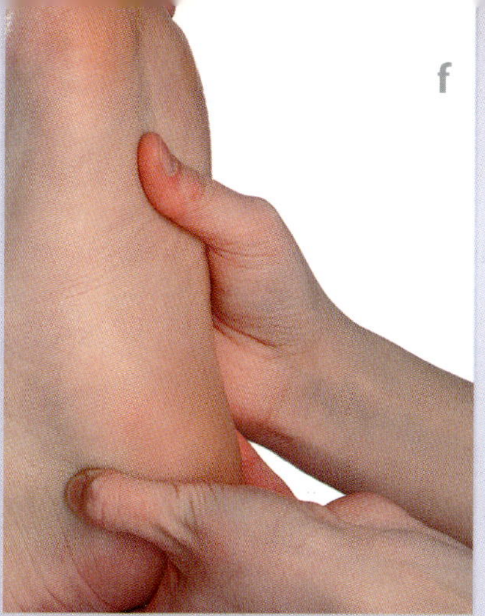

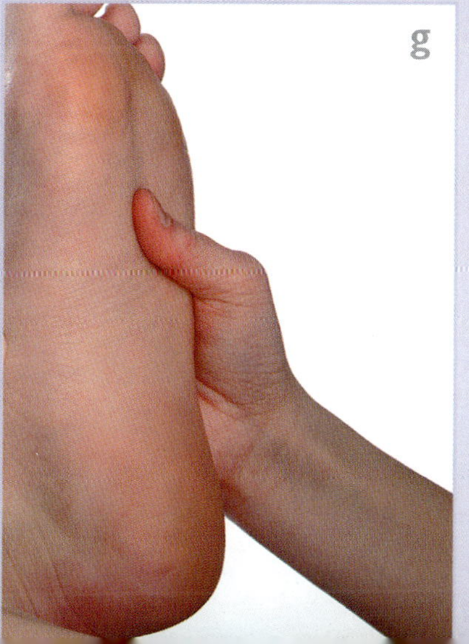

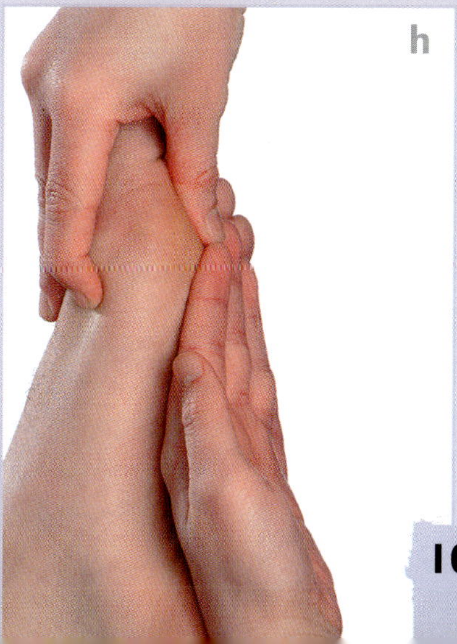

Using the multi-fingered technique, massage over the spine reflex running vertically from the plantar aspect to the dorsal but only treating the immediate area of the reflex. Travel from the coccyx to the top of the big toe and return (i, j).

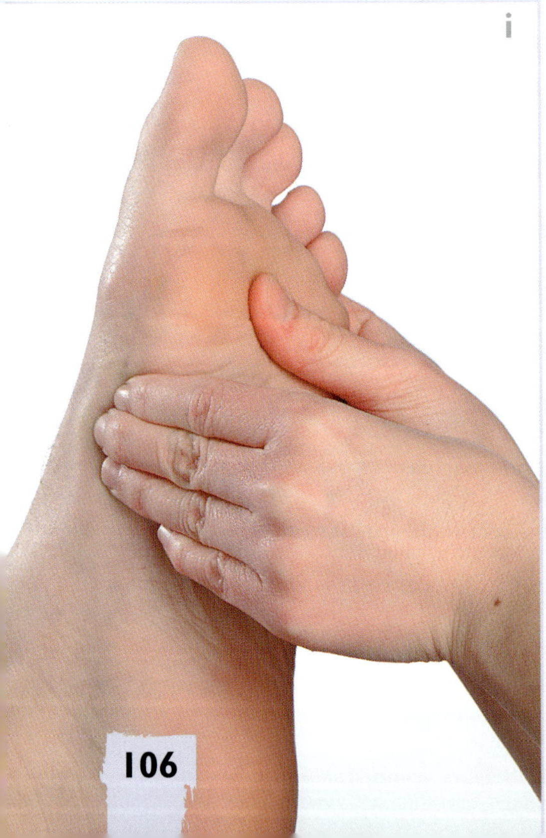

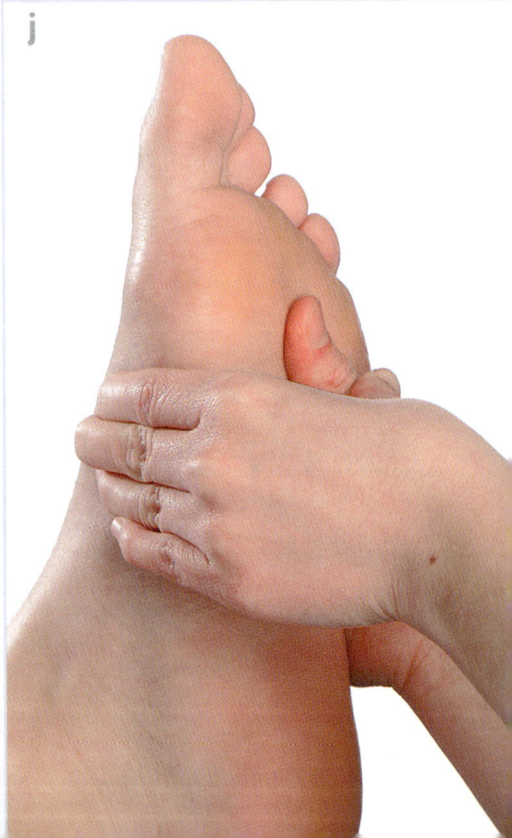

Thumb-walk across the heel from the medial to the lateral edge and back again, paying particular attention to the sciatic nerve area. You may need to apply a deeper pressure on this area. As it can be quite spongy and hard to work, gauge the amount of pressure needed by using your intuition and any reaction from the recipient.

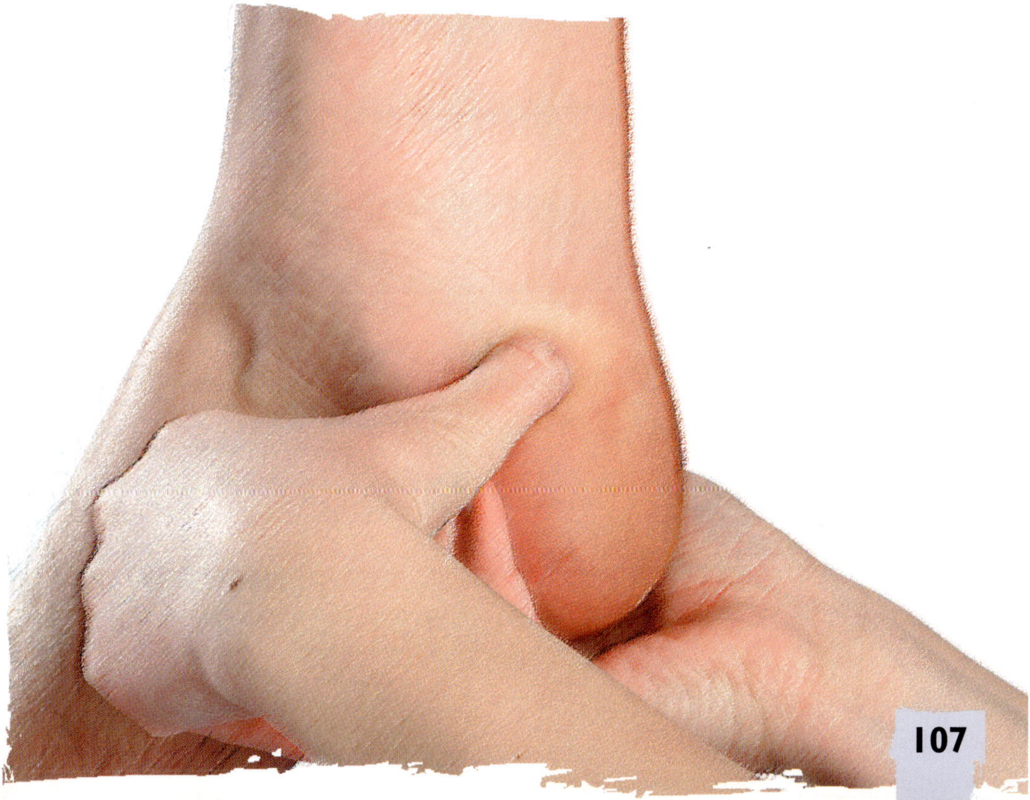

Water retention

At certain times in our lives we may experience swollen ankles, or feel as if we are carrying a little extra fluid and/or toxins. This routine is designed to stimulate the excretory system and improve the circulation of liquids within the body.

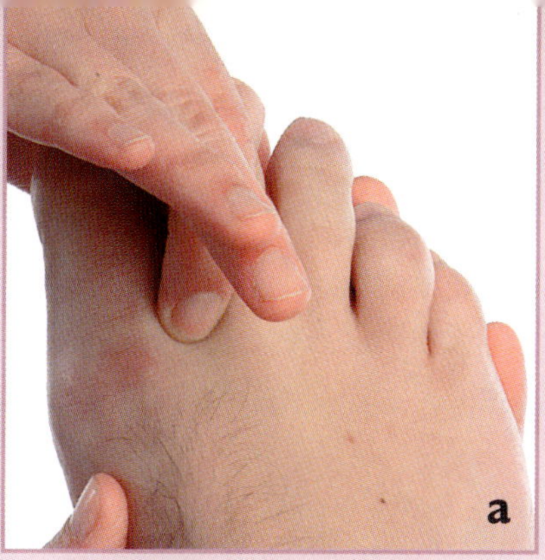

a

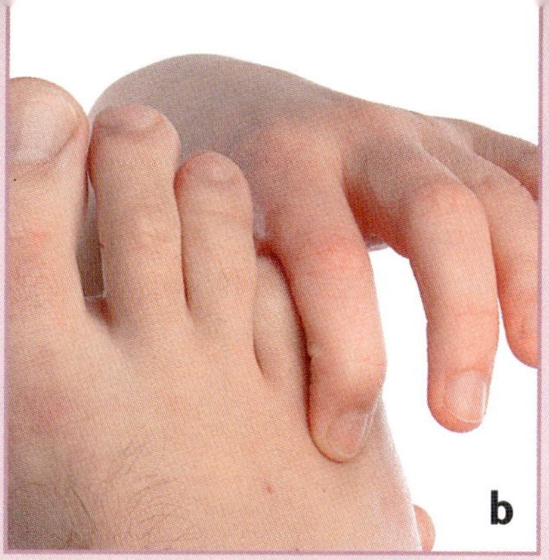

b

Follow the lines between each of the toes using the finger-walking method, working from the medial to the lateral edge and back in again. Work the line from between the base of the toes to the mid line of the dorsal aspect of the foot (a, b).

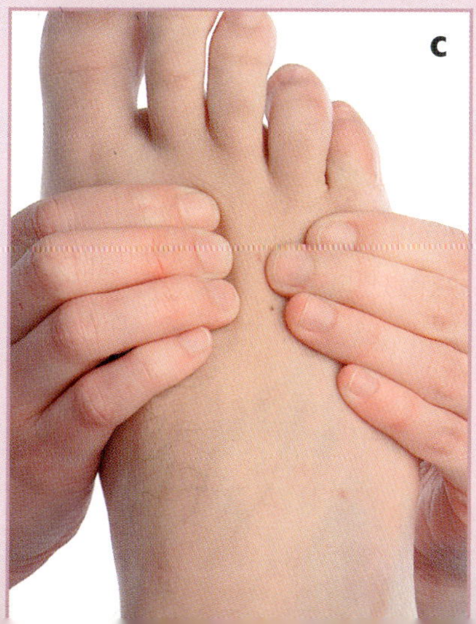

c

Using both hands and the multi-finger technique, work to the centre of the dorsal aspect of the foot, taking care not to nip the skin (c). Cover the whole of the dorsal aspect, stopping below the ankle joint, and repeat three times.

Working diagonally across on the plantar aspect, thumb-walk from the mid line of the foot up to the diaphragm line. Travel from medial to lateral edge, returning inwards on completion (d, e, f, g).

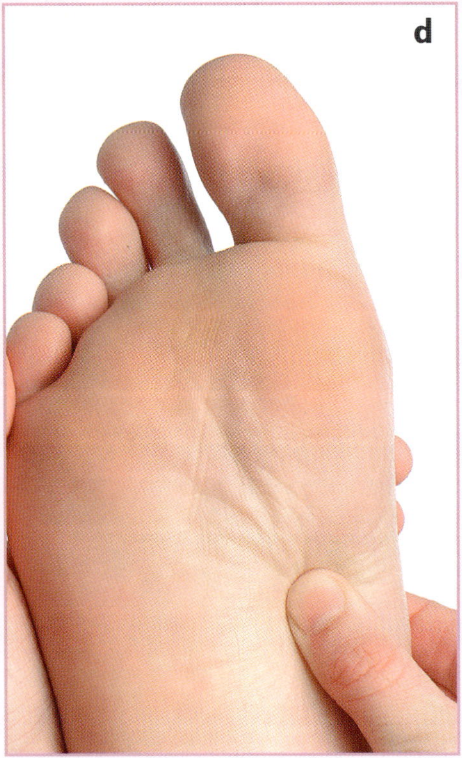

d

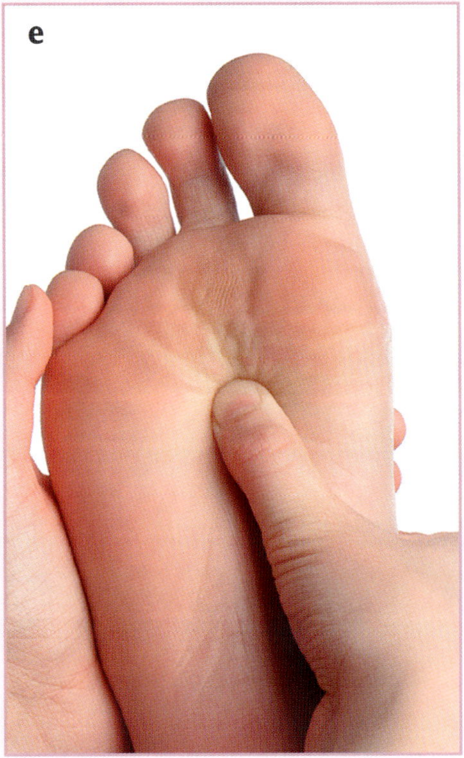

e

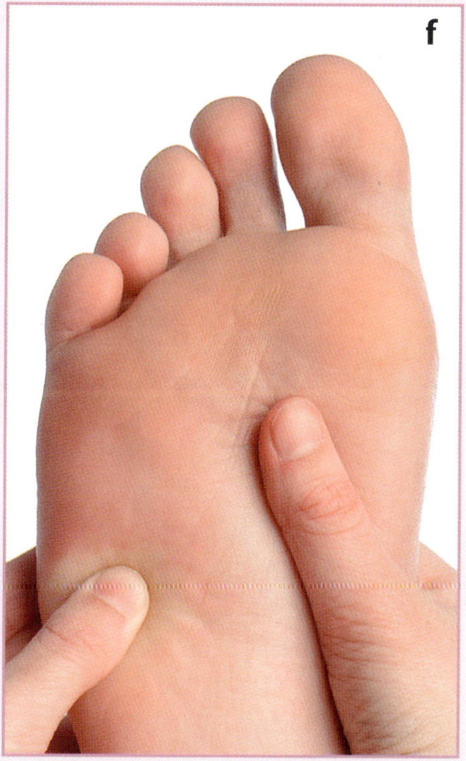
f

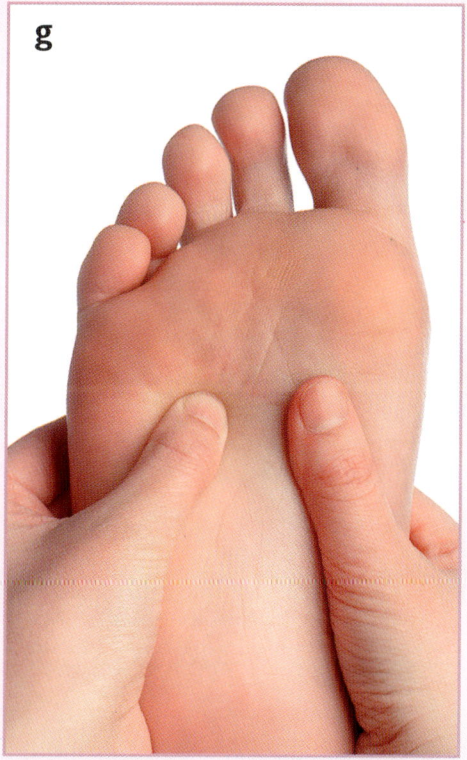
g

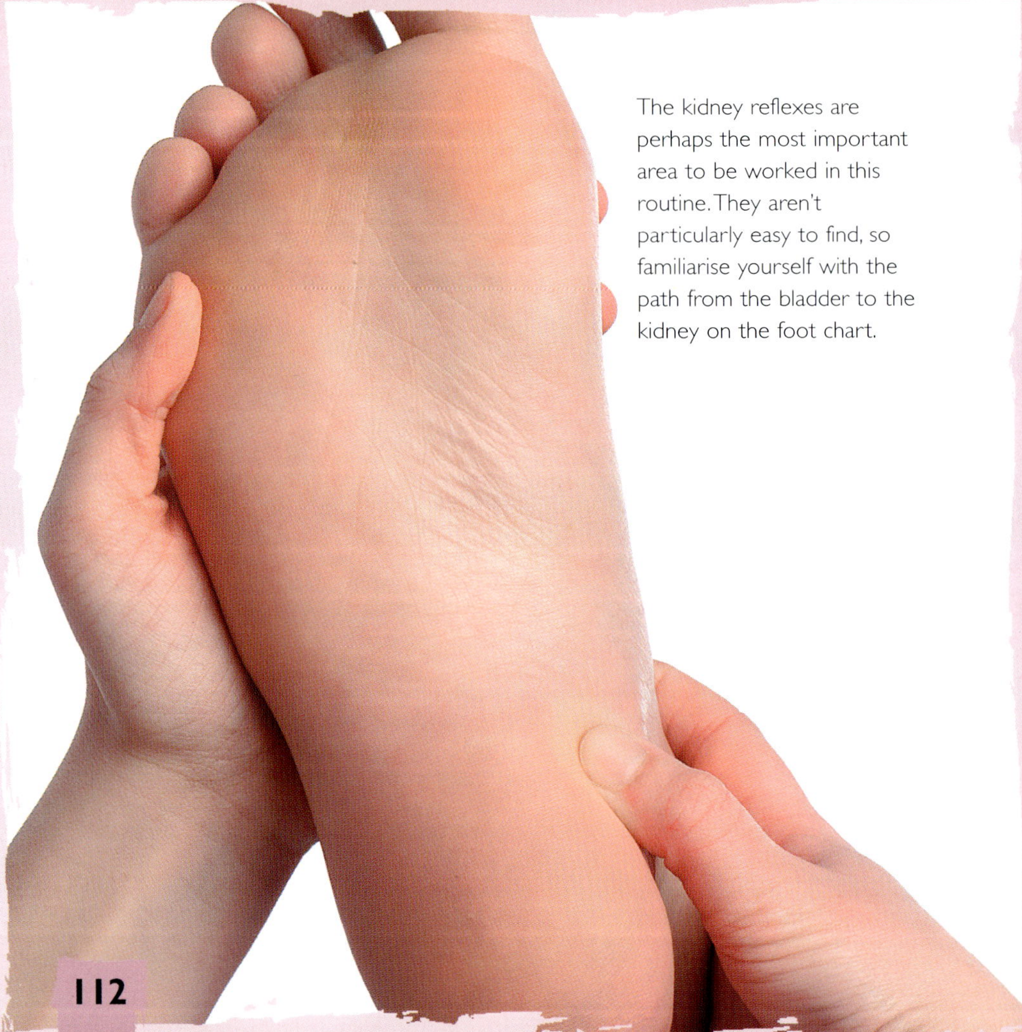

The kidney reflexes are perhaps the most important area to be worked in this routine. They aren't particularly easy to find, so familiarise yourself with the path from the bladder to the kidney on the foot chart.

Work three times over the bladder reflex, thumb-walking diagonally from the medial edge onto the plantar aspect of the foot (h). Work up and along the trajectory of the ureter reflex to the kidney and adrenal point. The easy way to recognise the correct position is to check that your thumb corresponds with the bone on the lateral edge that marks the waistline and that it is also in line with the middle of the second toe. Rotate on the kidney/adrenal reflex gently but firmly (i).

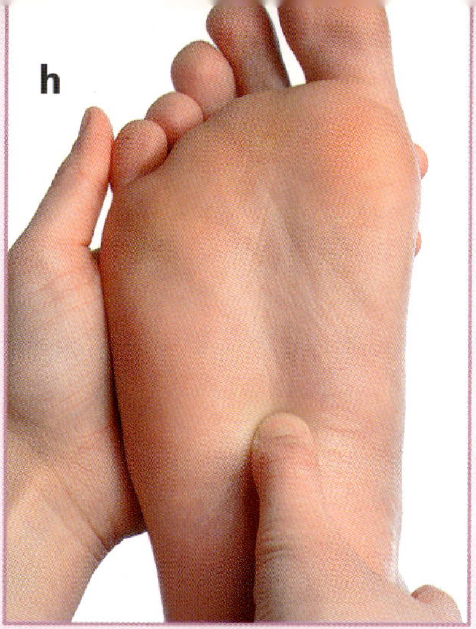

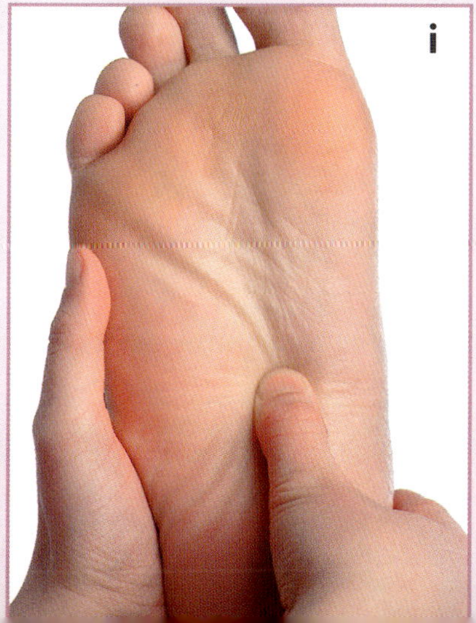

The next part of the routine concentrates on and around the ankle and is best avoided during the first stages of pregnancy as a precautionary measure, with care and light pressure being used in the later stages of pregnancy to alleviate any fluid retention that may occur.

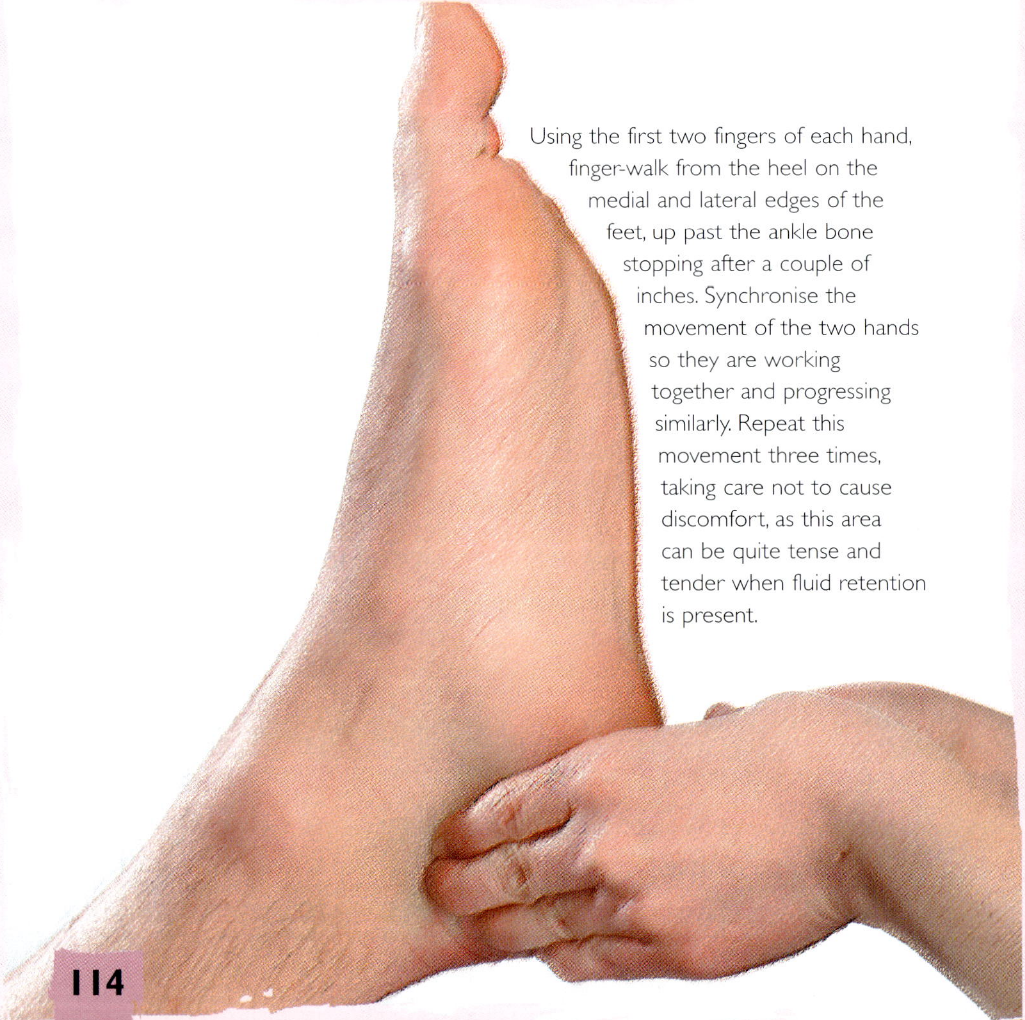

Using the first two fingers of each hand, finger-walk from the heel on the medial and lateral edges of the feet, up past the ankle bone stopping after a couple of inches. Synchronise the movement of the two hands so they are working together and progressing similarly. Repeat this movement three times, taking care not to cause discomfort, as this area can be quite tense and tender when fluid retention is present.

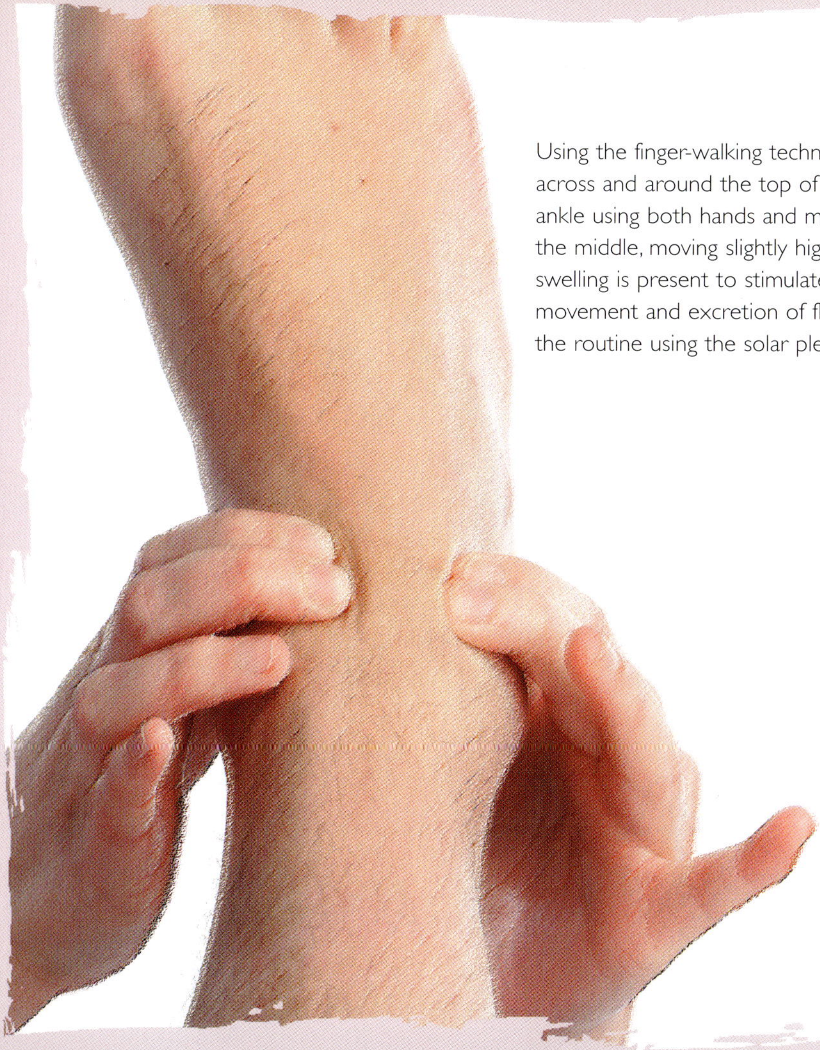

Using the finger-walking technique, work across and around the top of the ankle using both hands and meeting in the middle, moving slightly higher if swelling is present to stimulate the movement and excretion of fluid. End the routine using the solar plexus hold.

Reproductive AREAS

This routine is designed to help balance hormones within the body, aiding the menstrual cycle, the menopause and fertility, while also balancing male hormones and alleviating any prostate problems.

WARNING

This routine should be avoided during pregnancy. However, reflexology treatment during this time can be beneficial and helps to nurture both mother and baby throughout pregnancy and the birth process.

It is also wise to avoid this routine on the first day of your period if they are known to be heavy and/or painful.

Begin the routine with the relaxation routine as this is an important part of balancing hormones and the body as a whole, and is especially important if using this routine to improve fertility.

Thumb-walk vertically from the diaphragm line up to the base of the big toe on the plantar aspect of the foot, ensuring that you cover the thyroid reflex. Work from the medial aspect to the point between the big toe and the second toe, returning back to the medial edge.

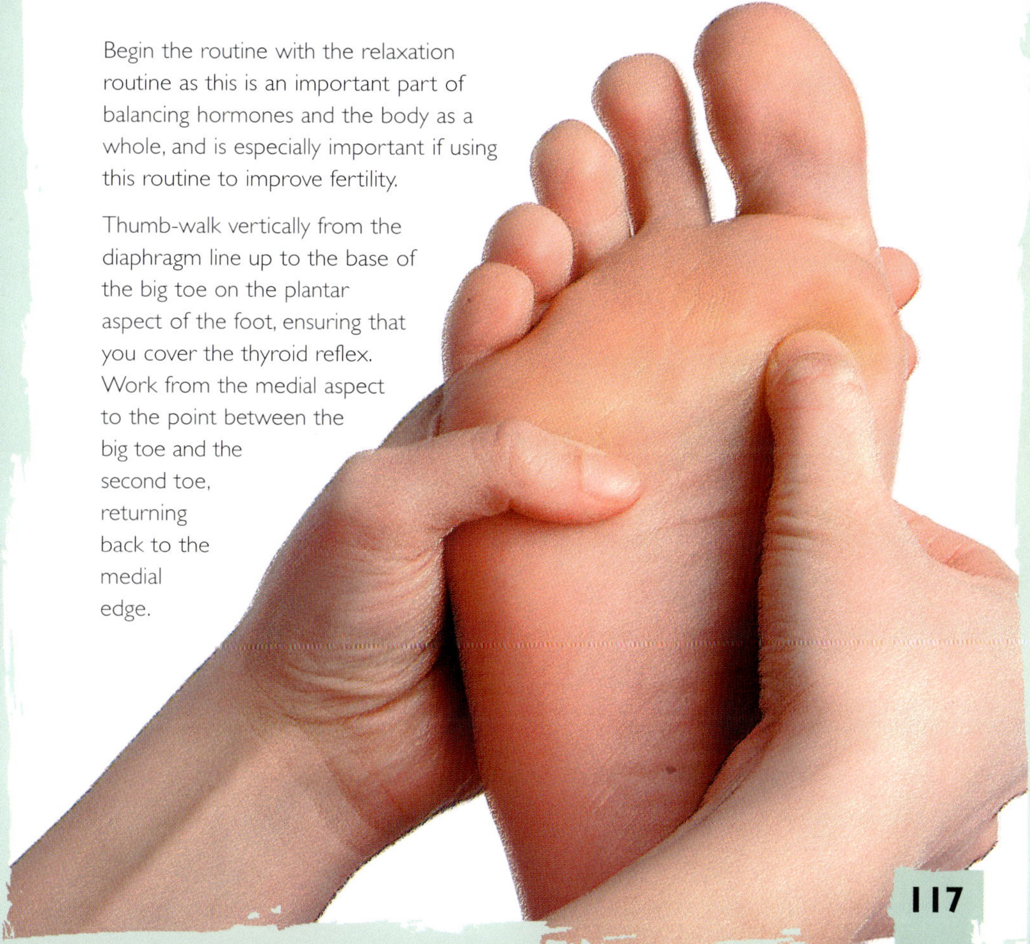

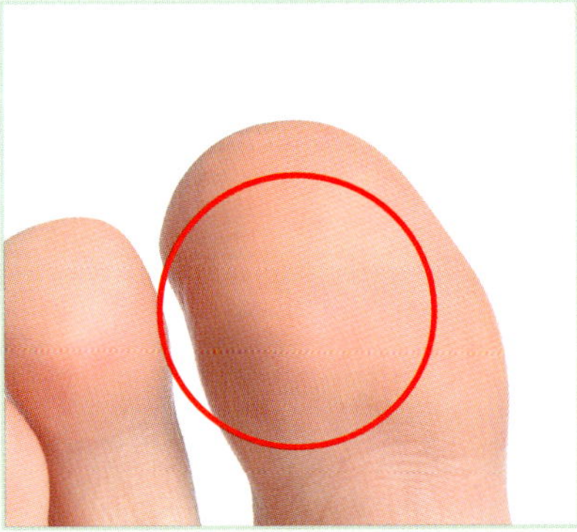

Hook in on the pituitary gland reflex three times. This is located underneath the mound characterised by a whorl, a gathering of lines shaping a circle on the skin. The reflex is usually quite tender so be aware of any reaction from the recipient.

The next reflexes to work are the ovary and uterus, testes or prostate. These are located underneath the ankle bone on the medial and lateral sides of the feet (a). It is probably best to refer to the foot chart to see the exact location. Work these areas by finger-walking in the direction from the heel to the leg; begin by working the uterus/prostate reflex first, then moving across to the ovary/testes reflex (b).

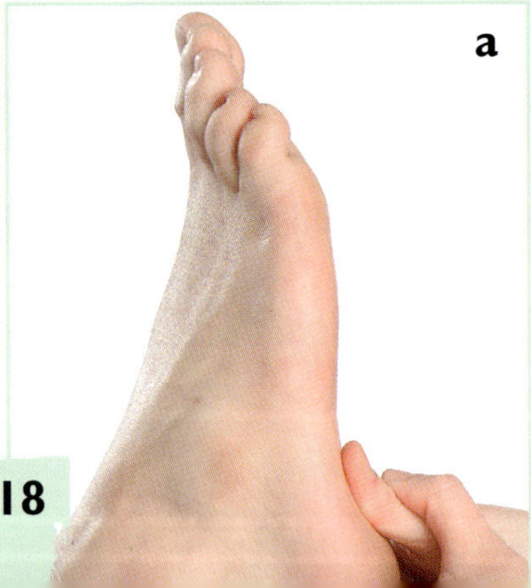

a

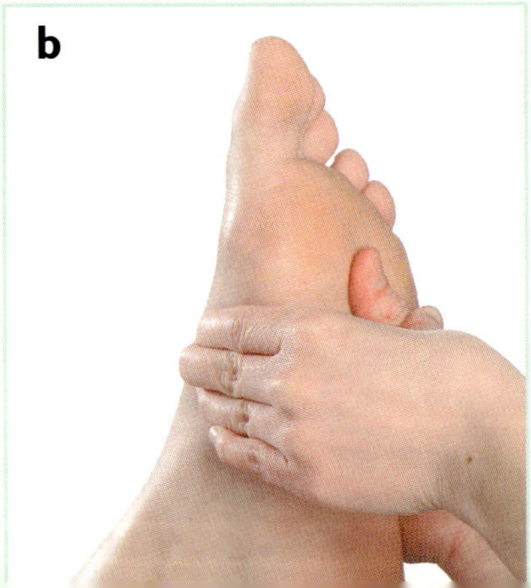

b

Use both hands to finger-walk across the Fallopian tube/vas deferens reflex on the dorsal aspect of the foot in to the middle, taking care not to nip the skin (c).

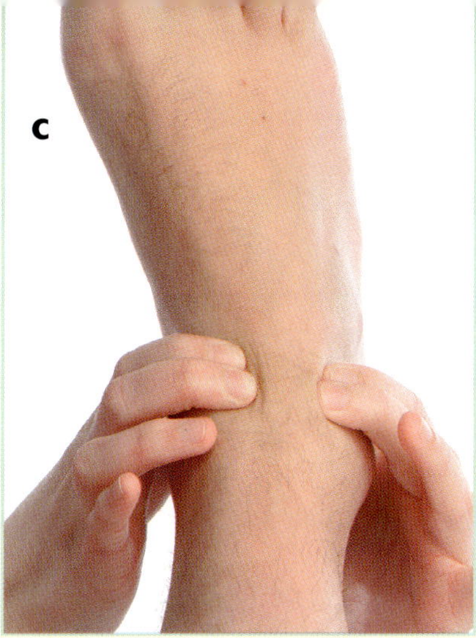

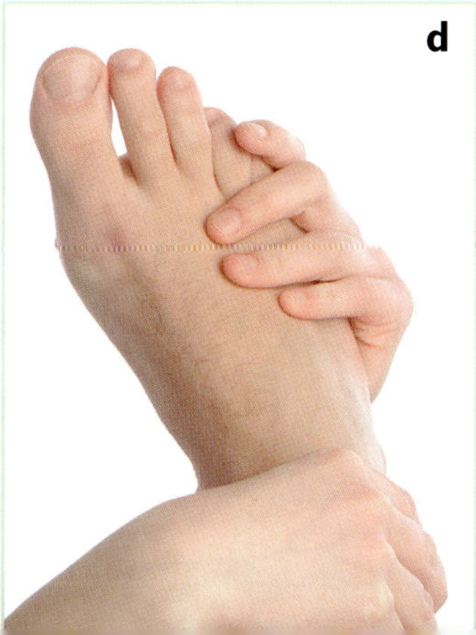

Hold the uterus/prostate and ovary/testes reflexes with your thumb and forefinger from underneath the ankle and briefly rotate towards the big toe (d).

Repeat the rotation with your hand over the top of the ankle, still holding the reproductive points.

Thumb-walk horizontally across the plantar aspect of the heel, working from the medial to the lateral edge, returning when the bottom of the heel has been reached.

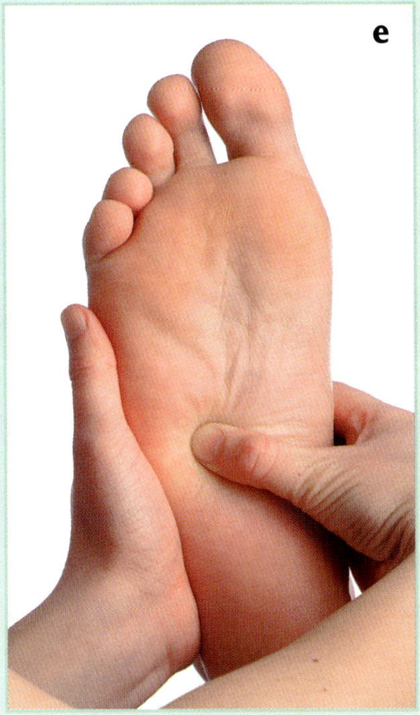

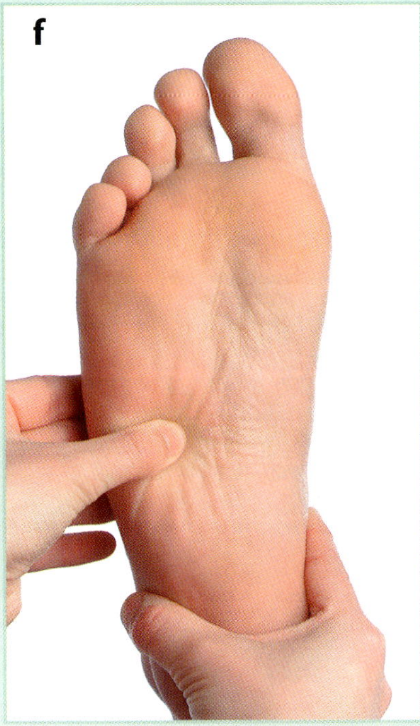

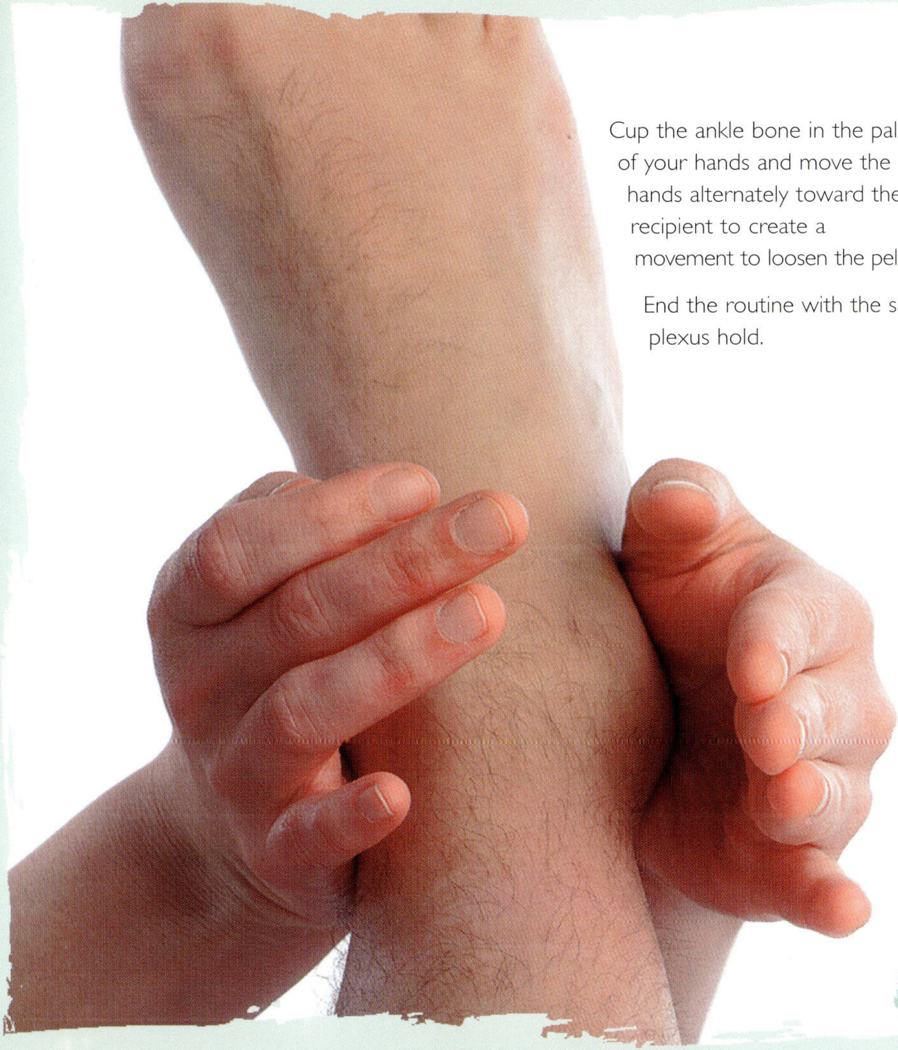

Cup the ankle bone in the palms of your hands and move the hands alternately toward the recipient to create a movement to loosen the pelvis.

End the routine with the solar plexus hold.

Frequency of TREATMENTS

The frequency of sessions is an important consideration in reflexology. Certain physical responses develop over time and this should be accounted for in any course of treatment.

In a lot of cases, an improvement is felt almost immediately, but it can take a few days before a balance has been established. Therefore, it is good practice to allow a break of two to three days between treatments if the condition is persistent, with a longer gap if the need for reflexology is not so great.

The routines that are listed in this book may be used to help combat stress and tension while also balancing the body as a whole. The techniques discussed use most, if not all, of the reflexes on the feet. With these routines, you will be able to adapt and change the reflexes worked as you feel necessary in order to treat other specific problems or conditions. Trust your intuition when performing reflexology. You may feel drawn to a specific reflex or find yourself initiating a new technique while working the feet. This is perfectly acceptable and is a natural part of working with the body's energy.

These routines are easy for the beginner to use. If you feel you have an affinity with the work or are interested in becoming a practitioner, it is essential that you find a qualification course to develop your knowledge further.

Energy MOVEMENTS

Many people are able to feel the transfer of energies while giving or receiving reflexology treatment.

Energy movements can be felt in many ways, most notably through temperature changes about the person or within the room. A tingling sensation may be felt travelling around the body of both parties involved. Sometimes there is a rushing sensation from the reflex point being worked to the relevant location within the body itself, which can manifest itself as a twitch. The energy felt during treatment is channelled to help balance the body and clear any stagnation that may have occurred as a result of illness, trauma or periods of stress.

This energy can often make the practitioner feel quite drained, either through intensity of the energy or as a result of opening themselves up to the channelling. The practice of yoga, t'ai chi, meditation, and visualisation improves the effectiveness and ability to open the self to directing the energies, as well as developing a spiritual sense of self.

Insider tips

As a holistic practice, reflexology can help the mind and body. Alongside traditional medical procedures, you may find that reflexology can assist certain physical conditions.

* When treating eczema and psoriasis, it is important to concentrate on the liver, lymphatic, kidney and adrenal reflexes, as well as on relaxation techniques.

* When an individual may be encountering problems with an unexplainable inability to conceive, it is a good idea to concentrate on a few key areas when giving reflexology as well as encouraging overall relaxation. Obviously, the reproductive and general relaxation routines would be ideal as a basis for regular treatment. Other important areas to pay attention to would be the thyroid, kidney, and lymphatic reflexes.

* Slight differences in the thyroid reflex may be found when treating women going through the menopause, which reflects the changing balance of the hormones.

* The pancreas reflex is very often affected during periods of grief, feeling hard and showing tenderness which eases as the process evolves. This is a physical manifestation of difficult emotion, and needs sensitive and flexible treatment.

* During pregnancy many reflexes on the feet change as gestation evolves. As the foetus develops, it is sometimes possible to see its progress as a shapely

swelling on or around the ovary, uterus, or bladder reflexes. The plantar aspect sometimes changes and shows a diagonal red swelling across the abdominal region as the pregnancy evolves, while the pancreas reflex also alters in texture.

* When someone is experiencing cystitis or thrush there can be a gathering of crystals on the plantar aspect, usually located on the bladder reflex close to, or on, the opening of the ureter. It can be quite a tender area, but light work on this area generally improves the condition.

* Frequent and persistent attacks of tonsillitis can be linked to the digestive system being out of balance. It is beneficial to concentrate on the ileo-caecal valve reflex, which may feel congested and/or tender. Follow on by working on the small and large intestine reflexes, the spleen, liver, lymph, and kidney reflexes. The ileo-caecal valve is also a prominent reflex to work to ease symptoms of food intolerances and allergies.

* When experiencing back problems, tension and pain, it is best to work not just the area of the spine giving the most aggravation but to include working the length of the spine, the hip and pelvis reflexes, neck and shoulders, the knee, and to try gently loosening the ankles, using the methods shown in the techniques section. When experiencing acute neck tension and problems, the bottom of the spine can also be affected as the tension spirals down and vice versa, so try paying attention to the whole length of the spine to alleviate the problem.

* On some occasions, the recipient may experience cramp during treatment. This can indicate poor circulation but more often than not, points to a recent emotional upheaval and/or a period of acute stress. Pushing the foot back toward the body can ease the cramp, so that the big toe is pointing to the head – remember to be firm but not over-zealous.

A therapy for LIFE

The importance and relevance of complementary therapies in modern life is being much more widely recognised by the public and institutions alike.

Reflexology, in particular, seems to be a therapy that most people find more approachable than others, with many people trying the therapy for the first time at natural health fairs or being introduced to it on the recommendation of a friend.

As well as being beneficial for health and well-being, the time spent in a reflexology session allows for personal reflection upon emotional or important issues. As our pace of life threatens to deluge and cloud our sense of self, this is one way of bringing focus and balance back to our everyday life.

The purpose of this book is not only to introduce this beneficial therapy to those who perhaps haven't had the opportunity to experience the delights of the treatment as yet, but also to bring reflexology into the home. Here it can potentially strengthen relationships, particularly within the family environment, allowing those closest to you to have some quality, tactile time in your company. It also reinforces the intensity of emotion felt for one another, nurturing the all important family bonds.

Reflexology is a positive experience, reinstating balance in life and freeing the mind and spirit. It often helps facilitate a change in life direction, promotes clarity of thought and changes of attitude to life and lifestyle.

The positive, life-affirming nature of this therapy emphasises its relevance for life and its need for inclusion and importance in society at large.

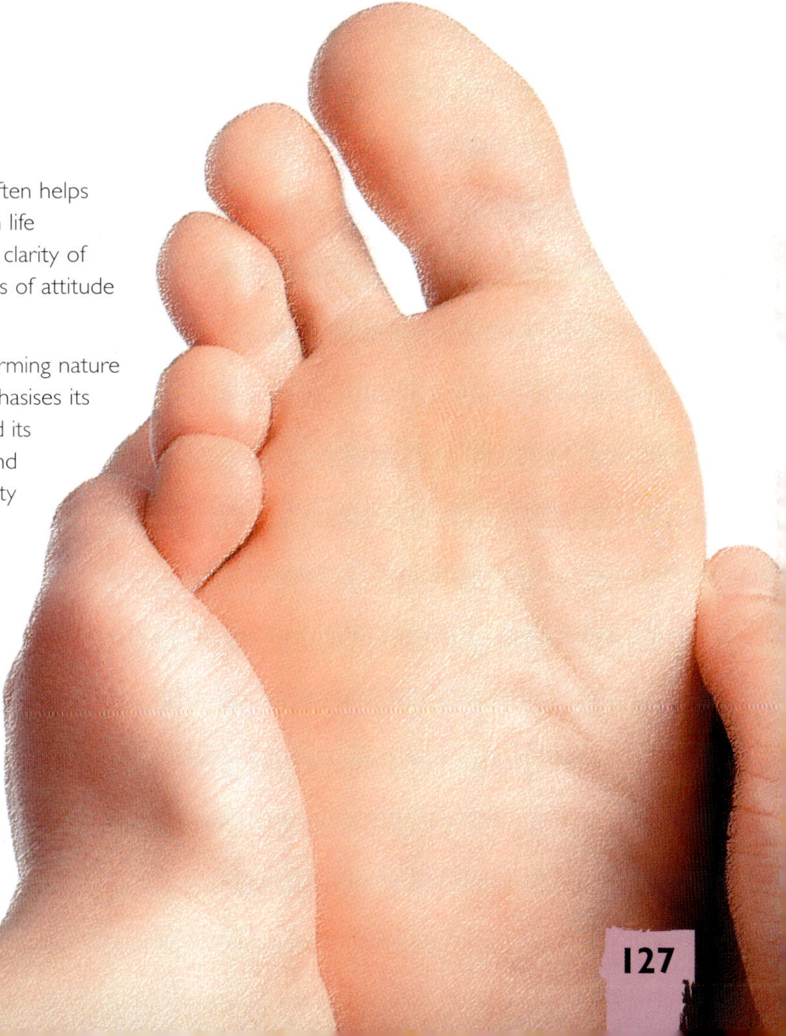

Addresses

Organisations

Association Of Reflexologists
Katepwa House
Ashfield Park Avenue
Ross-on-Wye
Herefordshire
HR9 5AX

Tel: 0870 567 3320

British Reflexology Association
Administration Office
Monks Orchard
Whitbourne
Worcester
WR6 5RB

Tel: 01886 821207

Books

Here are a few books to give you some more information on and around the subject of Reflexology.

The Reflexology Handbook: A Complete Guide – *Laura Norman & Thomas Cowan*

Reflexology: A Practical Introduction – *Inge Dougans*

Reflexology: The Definitive Practitioner's Manual – *Beryl Crane*

Stories the Feet Can Tell Thru Reflexology – *Eunice Ingham*

Stories the Feet Have Told Thru Reflexology – *Eunice Ingham*

Reflexology: The Definitive Guide – *Chris Stormer*

Language of the Feet – *Chris Stormer*

Reading Toes – *Imre Somogyi*

The Bodymind Workbook – *Debbie Shapiro*

Your Body Speaks your Mind – *Debbie Shapiro*

Heal Your Body – *Louise L. Hay*

Love, Medicine & Miracles/Peace, Love & Healing – *Bernie Seigel*

The Web Of Life – *John Davidson*

Traditional Acupuncture; The Law of the Five Elements – *Dianne M. Connelly*

The Wisdom Of the Body – *Sherwin B. Nuland*

Understanding Disease – *John Ball*

Molecules Of Emotion – *Candace B. Pert*

The Sickening Mind – *Paul Martin*